NATURAL
ALL AW
FORLA
WYERS

by J. Budziszewski

Edited by Jeffery J. Ventrella

ACW Press
Nashville, TN 37222

Except where otherwise indicated all Scripture quotations are taken from the Revised Standard Version of the Bible, Copyright 1946, 1952, 1971 by the Division of Christian Education of the National Council of the Churches of Christ in the U.S.A. Used by permission.

Cover Design by Hanon McKendry
Interior design by Pine Hill Graphics

Packaged by ACW Press
85334 Lorane Hwy
Eugene, Oregon 97405
www.acwpress.com
The views expressed or implied in this work do not necessarily reflect those of ACW Press. Ultimate design, content, and editorial accuracy of this work is the responsibility of the author(s).

Publisher's Cataloging-in-Publication Data
(Provided by Cassidy Cataloguing Services)

Budziszewski, J., 1952-

    Natural law for lawyers / by J. Budziszewski. — 1st ed. — Eugene, Ore. : ACW Press, 2006.

        p. ; cm.
        (Core curriculum series)

        ISBN-13: 978-1-932124-79-8 (perfectbound)
        ISBN-13: 978-1-932124-80-4 (hardcover)
        ISBN-10: 1-932124-79-9 (perfectbound)
        ISBN-10: 1-932124-80-2 (hardcover)
        Includes bibliographical references.

    1. Natural law. 2. Law—Philosophy. 3. Religion and law. I. Title.

K460 .B83 2006
340/.112—dc22   0605

Printed in the United States of America.

To Fr. James V. Schall, S.J.

Table of Contents

Acknowledgments

I gladly take this opportunity to express my deep gratitude to Bruce W. Green, first rector of the Blackstone Fellows, who first invited me to teach them; Jeffery J. Ventrella, their second rector, who suggested that I write this book for them; and to the Fellows themselves, whom it has been my privilege to introduce to the natural law.

1 | Introduction: Why Natural Law

The purpose of this book is to provide Christian law students with a clear, brief, and practical introduction to a tradition which is mostly ignored in law school, but which was once the foundation of legal education and is presently enjoying a renaissance. I offer the introduction not because I like old things, but in the conviction that this old thing happens to be true. The name of the tradition is the natural law.

At the root of this tradition is the idea that law is something more than a convention or a command of the sovereign power. The legislative decrees of governments depend on a "higher" law for their authority—a law which human beings discover rather than enact. Some people call this higher law "unwritten." If that makes you think of a cloudy something that cannot be known, change the metaphor; think of it as a law that is "written," but in something other than words. The tablet on which it is carved is created human nature—especially, but not only, the deep structure of the created moral intellect. This is what St. Paul meant when he said that its deepest requirements are "written on the heart" (Romans 2:14-15).

From the previous paragraph, already you may have noticed that what the natural law tradition calls "nature" is something different than what materialism calls "nature." Materialism imagines mere matter in motion, without meaning or design. What the natural law tradition has in prospect is created reality—the pattern of which inescapably reflects the purposes of its Creator, whether or not we choose to pay heed to it. Considering this fact, however, some people say that when the natural law was jettisoned from the legal curriculum, it was jettisoned for good reason. Let's consider this argument.

Is the Natural Law Tradition Obsolete?

You'll hear in law school that we live in a "pluralistic" political community in which controversial ideas like the pattern of created reality can no longer serve as the basis of public legal order. The natural law is obsolete. It might offend someone.

Actually, pluralism is just what makes the natural law so important. Let's consider the matter a little more carefully.

The term "pluralism" is used in three common senses. One common meaning is the distributed, bottom-up basis of social order. Human beings normally live not just in a community, but in a "civil society"—a community of communities, an association of associations, in which all sorts of social groups and institutions, like families, friendships, neighborhoods, churches, businesses, and labor associations coexist and cooperate. All that is true; in fact, the insight about pluralism in this first sense came originally from the natural law tradition itself. Just remember: Even though these different kinds of association involve different kinds of goods, respect for the moral basics is required in all of them. Principles of conduct like "Me first," "Just do it," and "Look out for Number One" are equally destructive whether we are thinking of a marriage, a city, or a social club. So pluralism in the first sense doesn't knock out the importance of the natural law; it underscores it.

Another common meaning of "pluralism" is the diversity of opinions and ways of life. This diversity too is a fact; the natural law tradition accepts it, in fact, insists upon it. People differ about all sorts of things, from little ones like whether a new road is needed, to middle ones like whether homeschooling should be regulated, to great ones like which way of life is best. But again consider: For disagreements to be fruitful, at least people must agree about how to regulate their disagreements. They must be of one mind about things like telling the truth, trying to be fair, and keeping away from each other's throats. In fact, they have to agree about certain things even to be *able* to disagree about other things. How can they argue if they can't come to terms about what they are arguing about? The deep agreements that even disagreements require are also matters of the natural law.

The third common meaning of "pluralism" is the social norm that diversity of opinions and behaviors should be *tolerated* rather than suppressed. That's true, but if you think it gets you off the hook of moral judgment, think again. Not even the staunchest advocate of tolerance believes that every evil should be tolerated; it is one thing to tolerate a false religion or bad taste in art, but who would propose tolerating rape or murder? True tolerance, then, doesn't mean tolerating everything; it means distinguishing correctly between the things that should be tolerated and the things that shouldn't. Rather than getting you off the hook of moral judgment, it puts you right on it. That's the quick version of the argument, but let's spell it out a little.

There are at least three reasons to recognize true tolerance as a virtue. One reason is that the legal suppression of evils can itself bring about certain evils. For example, if you tried to stamp out atheism by putting atheists in jail, you would be more likely to end up with a nation of frightened hypocrites than a nation of religious believers. This argument can be carried even further. I assumed a moment ago that religious belief can't really be coerced, but suppose that, through drugs or brainwashing or some such means, it can be. Would the resulting belief have any value? Not at all. As St. Hilary of Poitiers remarked, "God does not want unwilling worship, nor does He require a forced repentance."[1] A third reason for tolerance is that certain goods emerge

---

1. Hilary of Poiters, *To Constantius.* Cited in Lord Emerich Edward Dalberg Acton, "Political Thoughts on the Church," in *Essays in Religion, Politics, and Morality* (Vol. 3 of J. Rufus Fears, ed., *Selected Writings of Lord Acton*), p. 24.

more clearly through competition. For example, unless competing views are allowed to go head-to-head in debate, it may be difficult to tell which view is true and which is false. Notice that unless we understand that hypocrisy is bad, that knowledge of the truth is good, and that faith, by its very nature, is something that requires free assent, then arguments like the ones just given make no sense to us. We won't be able to make the moral judgments that true tolerance requires. But the understanding of such matters is also a concern of the natural law.

Is the Natural Law a Pipe Dream?

Someone might concede all that I have been saying but view it as beside the point. Your law professors, for example, may argue that the natural law is a pipe dream: That rational moral agreement is simply unattainable, not only about the details of morality but even about the basics. You may be tempted to agree. After all, in our dark times even the most elementary moral duties are often viewed as dispensable—duties like honesty, promise-keeping, honor to parents, faithfulness to spouses, and care for the young, old, and weak. A president is impeached for lying under oath. A physician is invited to kill his patient on television. Staggering numbers of fathers desert their minor children. Some marriage counselors say that a little adultery may be good for you. Professional psychology journals publish articles defending what used to be called child molestation but is now called "intergenerational intimacy."

The official line is that we should view such things not as instances of moral wrong but as instances of moral disagreement. There seems no limit to what people who claim to be morally upright may disagree about. Princeton University has given one of its highest honors to a philosopher best known for proposing a grace period during which parents may kill their infants.[2] Former Weather Underground terrorist Bill

---

2. Peter Singer, "Killing Babies Isn't Always Wrong," London *Spectator* (16 September 1995), pp. 20-22. Singer is the Ira B. DeCamp Professor of Bioethics, University Center for Human Values, Princeton University.

Ayers, who says that "I don't regret setting bombs," feels that "we didn't do enough," and would "not discount the possibility" of doing it again, is a professor in the School of Law, Northwestern University, as well as the School of Education, University of Illinois, Chicago Campus.[3] A plurality opinion of the Supreme Court has announced a "right to define one's own concept of existence, of meaning, of the universe, and of the mystery of human life," in effect declaring that the only moral principle is that there aren't any other moral principles.[4] Consider just that last example. Does the motto about liberty sound liberating? Then consider what the Court was talking about: Abortion. Translated into street language, its argument was that abortion must be allowed *because* everyone has a right to live by his own definitions of what "exists," what has "meaning," what the "universe" is, and what counts as a "human life." Consider the possibilities. A teen with a gun idly fires a shot into your bedroom window—because for him you don't exist. A sadist tortures your wife to death—because for him the meaning of her pain and fear is pleasure. A business rival wires your car to explode—because for him the universe is dog eat dog. An admirer of Adolf Hitler burns down the houses of your Jewish friends—because for him Jews aren't human life. There is no way in law or logic to distinguish the Court's argument for abortion from the other four arguments.

Is there a common moral ground? Can a moral consensus be recovered? Can we find our way to moral principles that are not only right for everyone, but in some way known to everyone? Against the natural law tradition, at least two schools of thought say "No."

One school says "No" on grounds that there *are* no moral laws that are right for everyone; what's right for you might be

---

3. Dinitia Smith, "Life With the Weathermen: No Regrets for a Life of Explosives," *The New York Times* (published, coincidentally, on the morning of 11 September 2001).
4. 505 U.S. 833 (1992).

wrong for me. This view is usually called moral relativism. Hardly any of your professors will be thoroughgoing, consistent moral relativists, though you may find a few who think they are; if they have been reading Judge Richard A. Posner, they may call morality "local" rather than "relative," but that means the same thing. Far greater numbers will be *selective* moral relativists. For example they may admit that moral laws about genocide or racial discrimination apply to everyone, but deny that moral laws about sex apply to everyone. By the way, that's a very large reservation. Not only does it wipe out every norm related to courtship, marriage, procreation, family life, and relations between men and women, but even before that avalanche is finished it sets off another. You'll find that most people who are confused about the connection between sex and procreation are also confused about the sanctity of life.

The other school of thought says "No" to the natural law because although it concedes that some moral laws might be right for everyone, it doesn't believe they are known to everyone. Rather it considers such laws obscure, full of exceptions and dilemmas, hard to recognize, still harder to understand— so problematic that we certainly cannot expect plain people to know them; experts—say, law professors—are called for. A few of the experts who take this view call it the natural law, but it isn't. I call it *mere* moral realism, with emphasis on the *mere*. The natural law, by contrast, is moral realism plus. It claims that the moral basics are not only right for all but at some level known to all.

Liberal legal thinkers—being either would-be relativists, selective relativists, mere moral realists, or something close— conclude that thick moral realism is all wrong. In their view, lawmakers should assume not the reality and necessity of the common moral ground, but the impossibility of a common moral ground. The only possible common ground is *amoral*, or as they say, "neutral." They say that laws and public institutions must award equal concern and respect for all possible goals, aspirations, and conceptions of the right way to live.[5] Only in this way, they think, can we escape the futility of endless arguments and carve out a public space in which people of every point of view can get along. The supposition here is that although the natural law is a mirage, neutrality is within the realm of possibility. Is that true?

Philosophers and social scientists increasingly recognize that neutrality is the mirage. Brian Barry remarks that anyone in political argument "must take his stand on the proposition that some ways of life, some types of character are more admirable than others." Gerald E. Frug explains that governmental value choices can be "disguised," but never eliminated. Joseph M. Boyle points out that any ground on which conflicts between moral perspectives can be arbitrated "will in fact be *some* moral perspective and the illusion that it is neutral will have the effect of disregarding the moral views of some citizens." Here is John Horton's comment on the notion that you can do anything you want as long as it doesn't hurt anyone: "What liberalism represents as the neutral requirement of preventing harm to others will be perceived by those with different conceptions of what is harmful as the enforcement of a morality they do not share." Gilbert Harman says simply that "you can't get something from nothing."[6]

To see how neutrality tries to get something from nothing, ask yourself whether there is a way to have equal concern and respect for the views of both the rapist and the woman he wants to rape. Of course there isn't. Either he gets his way and assaults her, or she gets her way and is left alone. Admitting this, some neutralists try to defend the rule of equal respect as merely a

---

5. For a generation, the chief architects of these ideas have been John Rawls, beginning with *A Theory of Justice* (Cambridge, Massachusetts: Harvard, 1971), and Ronald Dworkin, beginning with his article "Liberalism" in Stuart Hampshire, ed., *Public and Private Morality* (Cambridge, England: Cambridge University Press, 1978), and his book *Taking Rights Seriously* (Cambridge, Massachusetts: Harvard, 1978). Interestingly, Dworkin later criticized the neutralism of Rawls himself, and eventually recast his doctrine as a version of "mere" moral realism.

6. Emphasis added. See Budziszewski, *True Tolerance* (New Brunswick, N.J.: Transaction, 1992) p. 57.

starting point. For example they say that it's okay to thwart the rapist because he has already broken the rule: She respects his plans, but he doesn't respect hers. But that isn't true either. According to her plan, women in the neighborhood should be left alone. According to his, they should suffer his wish to molest them. She doesn't respect his plan any more than he respects hers. The real reason we condemn one plan and sympathize with the other is that they *don't* deserve equal concern and respect. There are certain ways in which a woman ought to be treated; she's right, he's wrong.

You may be thinking that although the neutralist's reasoning was confused, at least he reached the right conclusion. He did agree that rape should be prohibited. Yes, but that was just a lucky break, because it wasn't his neutralism that led him to the right conclusion. Presumably he had some dim apprehension of the natural law, which his neutralism obscured. More often, neutralists use neutralism *in order* to obscure the natural law. Here is an instance. Neutralists apply the principle of equal concern and respect not only to competing views of what ought to be, but to competing views of what is. For example, rather than finding out whether the child in the womb is a human being, they claim to award equal concern and respect to the view that he is and the view that he isn't. Since we can't say which view is true, they say, a woman should be free to carry the child or abort him, as she sees fit. But this doesn't follow. We don't say that it's all right to fire bullets into a crowded room because I might not hit anyone; we say that because I might hit someone, I'd better not. So instead of saying that "I can kill the baby because he might not be human," why don't we say that "Since he might be human, I shouldn't"? What this shows us is that would-be neutralists don't really award equal concern and respect to every view of what the baby is. Actually they award all their concern and respect to *one* view of what the baby is: Abracadabra, he's human if I think of him as human, otherwise not. This is a Harry Potter view of reality, an ontology for sorcerers. I can make the child an abscess, a blood clot, or a tumor—a dog, a frog, or a fish—whatever I want. It's all in my mind anyway.

We see that law and policy are never neutral, and neutralism functions merely as a license to be arbitrary. While claiming to reconcile competing views without deciding which one is true, it covertly supposes the truth of one of them but spares itself the trouble of demonstration. Where does this leave us?

It leaves us where we began. The only possible common ground is the common *moral* ground, the natural law. Make no mistake: It is a slippery common ground, slick with the mud of our evasions. But there is nowhere else to stand.

2 | The Meaning of the Natural Law

The previous chapter criticized neutralism, selective relativism, and other moral corrosives. Let us return to the thing that they are corroding. The natural law is the oldest tradition of Western moral thought—a *philosophia perennis*, or perennial philosophy, which has reasserted itself in age after age, all over the world, even under the most unpromising circumstances, despite the obscuring rivers of moral error, denial, and rebellion.

[margin note: TRIED AND TRUE.]

Natural law thinkers maintain that moral consensus can be recovered even in corrupted societies like our own, because people in general know more about the moral law than they realize—or more than they admit. The task of the moral persuader is not so much to explain to people what they don't know at all, as to dredge up and clarify their common moral sense. To put it another way, the immediate task isn't to convince people of the theory of the natural law—something they have probably never heard of. Rather it is to put them in touch with their own dim awareness of the natural law—something they already have. Of course, there is a place for teaching the theory of the natural law. After all, I'm teaching the theory to you! But your case is different. You're not the confused fellow citizen or fellow professional; you're the person who is being trained to reason with

[margin note: TASK OF THE MORAL PERSUADER.]

the confused fellow citizen or fellow professional. I certainly hope that you will be guided by the theory of the natural law, but that is quite different from referring to the theory of the natural law. By and large, people respond well to natural law concepts; they say things like, "I thought it must be something like that," or "I think I've always known that, but I didn't know I knew." On the other hand, they respond poorly when someone thumps on a big black book and declares, "The natural law says!"

One reason for the contrast between the two responses is that although the natural law was firmly embraced by the American Founders, who pledged themselves to "the laws of nature and nature's God" and declared "these truths" to be "self-evident," few Americans today have heard of it. All too often it is treated as a rarified study of academic philosophers, far from the concerns of ordinary folk. Yet its original aspiration was to set in order the moral understanding of Everyman: That universal common sense, "written on the heart," which can be denied and distorted, but never truly erased. To this day, that is its deepest goal.

Before we go on, let us take a moment to consider why it is that the natural law tradition has become so unfamiliar to most Americans. The question is difficult; no doubt there were many reasons. Surely, though, one of the most important is that the varieties of natural law theory which were known to the Founders had already been thinned and flattened by the intellectual movement which its proponents called the Enlightenment. The Enlightenment philosophers said they believed in the natural law, but discarded most of the equipment of the classical natural law tradition and denied its presuppositions. Though they inspired revolutions, over time their theories came to seem more and more implausible, and the very idea of the natural law was eventually dismissed. An intriguing interpretation of this blackout was offered by the nineteenth-century American writer Orestes Brownson, who said that the Founders built better than they knew. What he meant by this was that the institutions the

THE ENLIGHTEN-MENT DAMAGED IDEA OF NATURAL LAW

Founders developed were better than the theories they used to explain them; the institutions embodied deeper insights into the natural law than their explanations of the natural law did. As he saw it, the task facing the Americans of his day was to recover the classical natural law tradition, without which these insights could be neither elucidated nor preserved. If Americans failed in the task, then not only would the very idea of the natural law be discredited, but the institutions themselves, deprived of their necessary intellectual support, would suffer distortion and decline.

NEED NATURAL LAW TO PRESERVE OUR GOVERNMENT

What the Natural Law Is

When people ask, "What is the natural law?" they may be asking a number of different questions. Sometimes they are asking about the natural law *per se;* sometimes about the natural law *tradition;* sometimes about natural law *theory;* sometimes about the *content* of the natural law; sometimes, especially in law schools, about the *jurisprudential* views associated with the natural law tradition; and sometimes about the *term* "natural law"—why the natural law is called "natural" and why it is called "law." We will find it convenient to discuss each of these questions in turn.

The natural law *per se* is the foundational principles of right and wrong which are both right for all and at some level known to all—taken either by themselves (the first sense of the term), or together with their more obvious corollaries (the second). Not all of the corollaries of the natural law are obvious. Indeed, some of its remote implications may be recognized by only those few who have the requisite experience, acuteness, and discernment. It's also helpful to distinguish between truths which are obvious "in themselves" and truths which are obvious "to us"; the self-destructiveness of drunkenness is obvious in itself, but it may not be obvious to the drunk. As clarity of judgment aids probity of life, so probity of life aids clarity of judgment.

NATURAL LAW DEFINITION ① RIGHT FOR ALL ② KNOWN TO ALL.

The natural law *tradition* is the ancient and continuing project of disentangling the law written on the heart of man from

NATURAL LAW TRADITION DEFINITION

the evasions and subterfuges of men. In a thousand ways we human beings have dimmed and weakened the goods built into the order of creation, so this project requires labor. The labor is hardest when we are dealing with the remote implications of the natural law, easiest when we are dealing with its more obvious corollaries. "Easiest," however, doesn't always mean "easy." I may know that taking my neighbor's goods is wrong, yet tell myself that the people in the other tribe aren't neighbors; I may know that deliberately taking innocent human life is wrong, yet tell myself that my victim isn't human. Notice that even our excuses betray knowledge of the natural law. In the first place, nobody excuses his deed unless he knows there is something to excuse. In the second place, the only way to rationalize breaking a rule is to appeal in a dishonest way to the rule itself.

NATURAL LAW THEORY DEFINITION   A natural law *theory* is an explanation of the relations among goods, virtues, formal norms, and everyday moral rules—such as the good of friendship, the virtue of courage, the formal norm of treating equals equally, and the everyday rule "Do not steal." Natural law theories also explore such things as how we know the natural law, how our knowledge of it is clarified or obscured, and how its authority is rooted in God. Specialized branches of natural law theory consider the natural foundations of human institutions such as marriage, family, and government, and of human practices such as lawmaking, teaching, and medical care. Although the various natural law theories disagree about technical points, they all agree that the foundational principles of morality are right for everyone, that by the ordinary exercise of human reason they are known to everyone, that they closely parallel the contents of the Decalogue, and that their authority is rooted ultimately in God.

CONTENT OF NATURAL LAW   In identifying the *content* of the natural law with the Decalogue, or Ten Commandments, a few qualifications are in order. I don't mean that people know the natural law by reading the Bible, but that the Bible confirms the natural law that is dimly known everywhere. People in every place and time recognize that it is good to honor parents, wrong to commit adultery,

RELATIONSHIP BETWEEN BIBLE AND NATURAL LAW

and so on, even though they may fudge the details, and even though they may not live up to them. Again, I don't mean that ritual and historical parts of the Decalogue belong to the natural law, but only that its moral parts do. Take the Sabbath commandment; a mind unassisted by special revelation can see that times should be set apart for the worship of God, but will probably not find anything special in the seventh day. Finally, I don't mean that the natural law includes only the explicit content of the Decalogue, for it also includes what the Decalogue presupposes, implies, and suggests. The prohibition of adultery, for example, presupposes the procreative partnership called marriage, implies that there is something sacred about it, and suggests a broader norm of sexual purity, and the natural law takes in these things too.

[margin note: NATURAL LAW INCLUDES WHAT THE DECALOGUE PRESUPPOSES, IMPLIES, AND SUGGESTS]

The natural law tradition is associated with a *jurisprudential* view that laws which violate the foundational principles of right and wrong are not laws in the strict sense, but enacted frauds, abuses of governmental authority, which cannot in themselves command the assent of conscience. For this reason, the great natural law thinker St. Thomas Aquinas went on to consider the grounds of disobedience. Blending the natural law with Christian theology, he distinguished between laws which are unjust because they are destructive to this-worldly well-being, and laws which are unjust because they are destructive to eternal well-being. Laws of the former kind[7] *may* be disobeyed, except perhaps where disobedience is even more harmful than the unjust law itself.[8] Laws of the latter kind *must* be disobeyed; there are no exceptions. Significantly, these include every order to violate divine law—including, preeminently, the Decalogue, which

[margin note: 2 KINDS OF LAWS.]

---

7. The three cases he considers are laws which are defective in author, laws which are defective in form, and laws which are defective in end—paraphrased, laws which exceed the authority of the lawmaker, laws which violate the norm "to each what is due to him," and laws which seek to further private interest rather than the common good.

8. The two cases he considers are scandal and disturbance. Scandal is the moral snare or pitfall caused by bad example. Disturbance is violence, disorder, danger, or confusion.

belongs to both the divine and the natural law. If the government commands you for instance to blaspheme, to murder, or to steal, you must refuse, even if the penalty for refusing is death.

The view that unjust laws are not really laws has also given rise to a *misunderstanding* of natural law jurisprudence. Some people think that if unjust laws are not really laws, then courts are obligated to overturn them—in effect making themselves super-legislatures. This does not follow, because the question whether a law actually is unjust is distinct from the question of who, in a constitutional order, should have the authority to declare that it is unjust. The former is a question of moral principle; the latter is a question of prudence, specifically, the application of prudence in the allocation of authority among the various constitutional powers. More than one view of the latter question has been entertained by natural law thinkers.

TERM NATURAL LAW — NATURAL EXPLAINA-TION.   Finally, how about the *expression* "natural law"—is the natural law really natural, and is it really law? We do well to call it natural because it is built into created human nature, including the deep structure of the created human intellect. This has already been partially explained, and will be explained more fully in subsequent chapters. We also do well to call it law. The classic explanation is due to Thomas Aquinas, who argued that everything truly worth the name "law" is an ordinance of reason (rather than naked will), aimed at the common good (rather than special interest), made by public authority (rather than private power), and promulgated or made known (rather than kept secret). The natural law possesses these qualities to an eminent degree, because it was decreed by the wisdom of God for the good of all His creatures, and made known to human beings by endowing them with rational minds which could reflect, in their finite way, the infinite wisdom of His arrangements in Creation.

LAW DEFINITION

What the Natural Law Isn't

The natural law is often confused with things that are not the natural law. These confusions are rife among both critics and would-be proponents. One side attacks straw men, and all too often the other side defends the same straw men. For this reason, no explanation of what the natural law *is* can be complete without a brief consideration of some of the things that it *isn't*.

Is the natural law the same thing as innate moral knowledge? Critics are fond of saying that the natural law concerns innate ideas, but that there aren't any innate ideas, therefore there isn't any natural law. Actually, hardly anyone in the natural law tradition has ever suggested that the natural law is innate. The reason is easy to see. If the natural law were innate, then we would all know it the moment we emerged from the womb, which is plainly not the case. How could the newborn know that he ought to honor his parents, when he doesn't yet have concepts of "honor" or "parents"? We can say this, however: The ability to recognize the fundamentals of right and wrong is part of the equipment of the normal adult mind. To put it another way, there are certain moral basics that you *can't not know*, even if you tell yourself that you don't. You don't know them just because they were taught to you, and you don't know them because you derived them from other bits of knowledge. They are known in themselves.

[margin note: INNATE MORAL KNOWLEDGE?]

Is the natural law the same as biological instinct? This mistake is rife among sociobiologists, homosexual activists, and other biological determinists. If an instinct is defined as an urge that we can't resist, then it's highly unlikely that human beings have any instincts at all. If on the other hand an instinct is defined as an urge that we can resist, then it's easy to think of cases where moral duty bids us to resist with all our might; for example, I might have an abnormal genetic predisposition to abuse of alcohol. The source of the common confusion between morality and instincts may lie in the fact that the natural law tradition refers to "natural inclinations" as somehow underlying the natural law. So it does, but the term "natural" always refers to our design, and it is crucial to get this right. A designer endows his design with features that enable it to fulfill his design purposes; it doesn't follow that *every* use of these features is consistent with these purposes. We

[margin note: BIOLOGICAL INSTINCT?]

humans are designed with an inclination called anger—an arousal state which is activated by apparent danger to precious goods, and intended for their defense. However, this natural inclination is intended to function in cooperation with wisdom. In other words, we should be angry for the right reasons, toward the right persons, and in the right way. Thus, the *proper use* of anger is a precept of the natural law, but anger *per se* is not a precept of the natural law.

CULTURAL UNIVERSALS?   Is the natural law the same thing as cultural universals? No. It's true that the customs of almost all times and places more or less acknowledge the natural law, but these customs are not the same thing as the natural law; they are merely evidence for it. Such evidence must also be taken with a grain of salt. We are created by God, but we are also fallen; the universal knowledge of moral basics contends with the universal desire to evade them. Consequently, the fact that some custom is found in every human culture does not prove that it conforms to the natural law.

MORAL LAW PORTRAYED IN THE BIBLE?   Is the natural law the same thing as moral law as known through the Bible? No. Biblical moral law acknowledges it, conforms to it, extends it, and clarifies the divine basis of its authority, but when we use the expression "natural law" we are referring to what can be known even apart from the Bible. You can think of biblical and natural law as two different ways in which God makes His moral requirements known. Theologians

GENERAL VS. SPECIAL REVELATION   call the former "general revelation"—what God reveals to all human beings. They call the latter "special revelation"—what God reveals to the community of faith. These two modes of revelation overlap; as we have seen already, the Decalogue is an equally good summary of both. Where the two modes of revelation do *not* overlap, even so, each illuminates the other. Biblical law illuminates the natural law by making many remote implications of the natural law clearer than they would have been through human reasoning alone; it also explains the means of salvation, which reason could never have figured out for itself. The natural law illuminates biblical law because it contains a number of moral principles which the Bible presupposes but does not make explicit, like the norms "to each what is due to him" and "benefits produce obligations." By showing us how far short of holiness we fall, a heightened consciousness of the natural law might even be said to prepare gentiles for the gospel, in roughly the way that the law of Moses prepared the Hebrew people. I am thinking of Paul's remark, "the law was put in charge to lead us to Christ that we might be justified by faith" (Galatians 3:24).

Is the natural law the same thing as the theories that philosophers construct about it? No, although this is also a common mistake. Writers often confuse critique of a particular theory of the natural law with critique of the natural law itself. There may be many theories of the natural law, but the natural law itself is one thing—just as there may be many theories of gravitation, but gravitation itself is one thing. The natural law is the reality which a natural law theory tries to describe.

Is the natural law the same kind of thing as the physical laws of nature? Some people think that when a physicist calls the principles of gravity "natural laws" he is speaking literally, but when a philosopher calls the principles of gratitude "natural laws" he is speaking figuratively. Actually the opposite is the case; the former expression is the figurative one and the latter is the literal. Why is that? Because law is among other things an authoritative command addressed to a being capable of understanding what is demanded, and of acting upon it for that reason. Stones do not know what is expected of them; they just do it. We know we are expected to show gratitude, though we may refuse. We see then that even a *what* is a subject of God's providence, but only a *who* can be a subject of His law.

Why This Matters

As we have seen, natural lawyers claim that the rock-bottom basics of right and wrong are the same for everyone, both as to rectitude and as to knowledge. Suppose they weren't; suppose they weren't right for all, or weren't known to all. Today, many lawyers, judges, and philosophers of jurisprudence believe that this is exactly the way things stand. What difference would it make if that were true?

If the rock-bottom basics weren't right for all, then moral reasoning and persuasion would be pointless. There would be nothing for them to be *about*. The truth about right and wrong would be what Oliver Wendell Holmes used to say that all truth was: "the majority vote of that nation that could lick all others." In fact it would be even less than that, for why follow the majority? The great moral debates would be nothing but discourses of idiots, full of sound and fury, signifying nothing.

If the rock-bottom basics weren't known to all, then even if moral reasoning and persuasion *were* about something they could never get anywhere. The reason? Dialectic works in one direction only. Reasoning moves from the known to the not yet known; persuasion, from the conceded to the not yet conceded. Without a common ground, the movement could never get started. There would be no place for it to begin.

3 | Pagan Sources of Natural Law Tradition

Considering that the natural law was the axle on which Western jurisprudence turned for centuries, it is amazing how thoroughly it has been purged from law school curricula and replaced by secularist ideologies—and how recently all that happened. The natural law tradition is presently enjoying a renaissance, of which this book is in a small way representative. To really understand your profession, however, you need to learn not only the meaning of the natural law in the abstract, but the historical sources from which natural law reasoning has drawn. I realize that you are preparing to be lawyers, not historians or philosophers, but a lawyer who does not understand the roots of jurisprudence is no lawyer at all. Here we begin a pair of chapters about these roots.

Antigone

It may surprise you that a Christian author begins a discussion of the roots of Christian natural law reasoning with pagan thinkers. This is not so strange; there is nothing Christian about thinking that God ignored the rest of the world while He was training the covenant people. Paul declared to the pagans of Lystra that although in times past, God allowed the gentile nations to walk in their own ways, even then "He did not leave

Himself without witness." The context shows that he is not speaking of human witnesses, but of a testimony built into the very pattern of His providence.[9] Because this testimony is dimly heard everywhere, Paul can introduce another pagan people, the Athenians, to the gospel by reminding them of what their own poets had said and of how their own altars were inscribed.[10] Considering all this, it would have been surprising if pagan thinkers had *not* caught a glimpse of the natural law.

"Pagan," however, is a broad category. Considering that the natural law is dimly known everywhere, why did the tradition of natural law *reasoning* take root only in the West? One great reason is the Greek invention of philosophy. Philosophy was not just another wisdom literature; it was a wisdom literature that attempted to proceed by rational investigation. Before we look at the Greek philosophers, however, let's glance at the *pre*philosophical roots of the natural law tradition—at how the dim universal knowledge of the natural law was reflected in Greek culture.

In a phrase of unforgettable poignancy, C.S. Lewis once described pagan mythology as "gleams of celestial strength and beauty falling on a jungle of filth and imbecility."[11] That is a good image not only for pagan mythology, but for pagan culture as a whole. We would be gravely mistaken to pass over the filth and imbecility, but we would be equally negligent to forget the celestial gleams. One such gleam fell upon the Greek tragedy *Antigone*. The heroine seeks to give her dead brother a proper burial, but the king forbids her because her brother was an enemy of the state. Antigone replies that there is another law higher than the king's, a law which came from the gods—no one knows when. She resolves to follow *that* law, not his.

Because of our own faith traditions, we are apt to overlook the strangeness of Antigone's claim in its context. The gods of the Greeks were not lawgivers like the true God, and the Greeks

---

9. Acts 14:16-17 (RSV).
10. Acts 17:22-23, 28.
11. C.S. Lewis, *Perelandra* (New York: Macmillan, 1965, orig. 1944), Chapter 16; in the edition cited, p. 201.

had no records of direct divine instruction. Unless Antigone has been reading Torah, then how has she learned of this law of which she speaks? Her words allude to a standard of decency and justice which does not depend on words, yet which impresses itself on us as law, and which somehow bears the stamp of an authority higher than our own. She has no name for it—but we do. She is speaking of the natural law.

Aristotle

When we do turn to the pagan philosophers, pride of place goes to Aristotle. In his *Rhetoric*, he actually quotes Antigone, calling attention to the unwritten law without which the written law cannot be understood. But he does much more than that. In the *Nicomachean Ethics*, for example, he distinguishes natural justice from conventional justice. The former is what really is just everywhere, whether people say it is or not; the latter is what people call just here and there, whether it really is or not. In his *Physics* as well as in other works, he makes clear that everything in nature has purpose and design—from the eye, the inbuilt purpose of which is to see, to the marital pair, the inbuilt purpose of which is to procreate and nurture the young, to the soul, the inbuilt purpose of which is to follow its distinctive potentiality, reason, which directs it to the truth. His most important contribution to the natural law tradition, however, is his approach to moral inquiry.

Aristotle began every discussion of ethical questions with the common moral sense of the human race—not the consensus of his own time and place, but of all times and places. At some points he spoke of the consensus of everyone everywhere, at others of the opinions of men whose exceptional wisdom everyone everywhere concedes, but either way, the emphasis is on what everyone has an inkling of already. When several opinions on a given moral subject are found in all times and places, he considered each of them. It might seem that this method falls prey to the fallacy called argument *ad populum*, illegitimate appeal to the prejudices of the crowd. But not all common opinion is prejudice, not every appeal to it is illegitimate, and the whole human race is a rather different crowd than the transient majority of people in my time. Moreover, Aristotle does not consider general opinions about matters that people in general know nothing about, like the density of the sun; rather he considers general opinions about matters that people in general do know something about, like what it is they want. And although he begins with common opinions, he never ends with them; he always subjects them to scrutiny.

Remarkably, even Aristotle's scrutiny of common opinions depends in a way on common opinions, for he doesn't simply shoot arrows at them from on high. He makes them interrogate themselves. By way of illustration, consider the place in the *Ethics* where he asks whether people regard anything as good in itself, as worth pursuing for its own sake, not merely for the sake of something else. One common opinion on the matter is that honor—praise from other people—is such a good. Very well, says Aristotle, let us address a question to the people who hold that opinion. Would they be satisfied if other people praised them for qualities they knew they did not have? The answer they actually give is "No." *That* sort of praise they find empty; it has no savor. But if they do give this answer, says Aristotle, then obviously they don't consider praise worth having for its own sake after all. They only think that they do. What they really find good in itself is not praise, but praiseworthiness. Once this fact is recognized, it changes the whole conversation.

As just described, the Aristotelian approach is very much the approach of all natural law thinkers. The idea is not to destroy the common moral sense, but to heighten, to elevate, to ennoble it, by forcing it to be honest with itself. I submit that if the New Testament is right about the hearts of fallen men—that a law is universally written there, but obscured by an equally universal reluctance to read the inscription—then this is precisely the right way to proceed.

God Himself appeals to preexisting moral knowledge. In commending His commandments to the Hebrews, He asks "what other nation is so great as to have such righteous decrees and laws as this body of laws I am setting before you today?"[12] If He had not already inscribed this same law on their hearts, His question would have had no point; they would have been unable to answer it. We may therefore paraphrase His inquiry, "Do you not see that this body of laws I am setting before you is a more perfect expression of what I have already made known by other means?"

I remarked earlier that Aristotle recognized that everything in nature has purpose and design. Today people say it is rubbish to talk about natural purposes, because we merely imagine them; purposes are in the eye of the beholder. But is this true? Take the lungs, for example. When we say that their purpose is oxygenating the blood, are we merely making it up, projecting our own wishes upon an empty screen? Of course not; the purpose is implicit in the design. In fact there is no way to explain the phenomenon of lungs *apart* from their oxygenation of blood. Suppose a young man tells me that he is not interested in having his blood oxygenated—he is more interested in using his lungs to sniff glue and get high. If I were to conclude that the purpose of *his* lungs must be getting high, you would think me a fool, and rightly so. He can't alter the purpose of his lungs just by using them for something else; he can only violate it.

Another objection is that even if there are such things as natural purposes, they are irrelevant. What *is*, people say, does not imply what *ought to be*. This argument also misses the mark, because a certain sort of *is* really does imply an *ought*.[13] If the purpose of eyes is to see, then eyes that see well are good eyes and eyes that see poorly are poor ones; that is what it *means* for eyes to be good. Moreover, good is to be pursued. In fact, the appropriateness of pursuit is what it means for *anything* to be good. Therefore, the appropriate thing to do with poor eyes is try to turn them into good ones. By the same sort of reasoning,

---

12. Deuteronomy 4:8 (NIV).
13. Concerning this point, see also chapter eight.

the appropriate advice for the glue-sniffer is "kick the habit." In short, we *ought* to respect the human design. Nothing in it should be used in a way that flouts its inbuilt purposes.

No one in the natural law tradition has made more effective use of Aristotle than the Christian thinker Thomas Aquinas, of whom I have much to say later. Some people say that by doing so, he "baptized" the old pagan. Ernest Fortin puts the achievement of St. Thomas in sharper perspective:

> Contrary to what has often been said, Aquinas did not baptize Aristotle. If anything, he declared invalid the baptism conferred upon him by his early commentators and denied him admission to full citizenship in the City of God. Instead, by casting his philosophy in the role of a handmaid, he made him a slave or servant of that City.[14]

In this way St. Thomas provides a model of how non-Christian sources should be used.

The Stoics

You may be wondering: Doesn't Aristotle's talk about a design that we ought to respect presuppose the wisdom, goodness, power, and authority of the Designer? It does, and therein lies Aristotle's great limitation. He recognized the design, but he failed to recognize the presupposition of design—the Designer. A later group of thinkers, the Stoics, in one way came closer. These later philosophers affirmed a divine mind which rules the universe, a mind of which the natural law is the expression. Having minds themselves, they thought, we ought to follow this law, and we ought to do so not instinctually, as animals do, but deliberately. Unfortunately, the Stoics suffered from several great limitations of their own.

---

14. Ernest L. Fortin, "St. Thomas Aquinas," in Leo Strauss and Joseph Cropsey, eds., *History of Political Philosophy*, 3d edn. (Chicago: University of Chicago Press, 1987), p. 271.

In the first place, the Stoics failed to recognize that mind MIND GOES WITH PERSONHOOD. and personhood go together—that every mind is *someone's* mind. Moreover, they failed to distinguish the divine mind from the universe it ruled, so the sense in which it did rule the universe remained unclear. Still worse, they were materialists, and being MIND IS DISTINGUISHED FROM MATTER materialists, they were unable to distinguish mind from matter; they imagined the divine mind merely as a finer sort of matter permeating the coarser sort which makes up the rest of the cosmos—something like dye dissolved in a glass of water. Finally, THERE IS FREEDOM they were determinists. Nothing in the universe is free, the human mind included. Thus, insist as they might that human beings should follow the natural law deliberately rather than instinctually, in the end they were unable to explain how the one way of following it is different from the other. At the end of their wandering speculations we are deep in the jungle, far indeed from that original celestial gleam.

Yet by common grace, the gleam never quite dies out, and the Stoics taught better than they knew. From time to time they gave utterance to insights far beyond what their faulty philosophy could have led them to by itself. It was through Stoic influence, for example, that Marcus Tullius Cicero wrote the following great lines, which sound almost Christian, and have been quoted by Christians since Lactantius:[15]

> True law is right reason in agreement with nature; it is of universal application, unchanging and everlasting; it summons to duty by its commands, and averts from wrongdoing by its prohibitions. And it does not lay its commands or prohibitions upon good men in vain, though neither have any effect on the wicked. It is a sin to try to alter this law, nor is it allowable to attempt to repeal any part of it, and it is impossible to abolish it entirely. We cannot be freed from its obligations by senate or people, and we need not look outside ourselves

---

15. Lactantius, *Institutes*, 6.8.

for an expounder or interpreter of it. And there will
not be different laws at Rome and at Athens, or different laws now and in the future, but one eternal and
unchangeable law will be valid for all nations and all
times, and there will be one master and ruler, that is,
God, over us all, for he is the author of this law, its
promulgator, and its enforcing judge. Whoever is dis-
obedient is fleeing from himself and denying his
human nature, and by reason of this very fact he will
suffer the worst penalties, even if he escapes what is
commonly considered punishment.[16]

These thoughts go beyond what Cicero's theory can explain.
They would have been impossible to achieve—had it not been
for the law that was written on his heart.

---

16. Marcus Tullius Cicero, *De Republica* (Loeb Classical Library, 1950), at 3.22.33.

4 | Christian and Jewish Sources of Natural Law Tradition

In the previous chapter I surprised you by discussing pagan sources of natural law reasoning. We turn now to a more Christian source, the Holy Scriptures of both the Old and New Testaments. Because the Old Testament is the Bible of our "older brother" tradition, Judaism, the chapter concludes with remarks about the place of the natural law in rabbinical tradition.

Not Without Witness

By Jesus' time, pagan thinkers had long used the term Logos, which we translate Word, for that mysterious divine principle on which the whole cosmos depends, in which it coheres, and because of which the intellect can grasp it. John, in the prologue to his Gospel, identifies this unknown god of the philosophers with Jesus Christ Himself. In Him we see that the Ground of Being is not an abstract principle but a personal Being, not a part of the cosmos but its Creator, whose Word alone causes it to be.

GOD OF PHILOSOPHERS
= LOGOS =
THE WORD =
JESUS!

Such allusions to pagan knowledge unsettle some Christians. They think it impossible that nonbelievers should know anything whatever; the very idea of general revelation seems un-Christian to them. They think it is unbiblical to believe that God has revealed anything outside of the Bible. Remarkably, the Bible itself

says just the opposite; in fact it maintains that in various ways, God
has revealed certain things about Himself to *all* human beings.
Even those who have never heard of the Bible have "heard" them,
and even those who deny having heard, have heard; they merely
put their fingers in their ears. These things include not only God's
reality but also His most basic moral requirements.

Scripture alludes to at least four modes of general moral
revelation. Recalling Paul's remark to the people of Lystra that
God has not left Himself without "witness" among the nations,
I call them the Four Witnesses: Deep conscience, designedness
in general, the details of our own design, and the natural consequences of our deeds. Let's consider each one in turn.

FOUR WITNESSES

The Witness of Deep Conscience

According to the prevailing secular view, conscience is something pumped into us from outside. That's not wholly false; the
surface layers of conscience really are modified by socialization.
That's one of the reasons why good moral teaching is important.
But consider how moral teaching really works. At each stage of
development, the reason you can teach a child something is that
he knows something already, apart from your teaching. What you
are doing is awakening it, eliciting it, making it stronger.

AWAKEN, NOT TEACH CONSCIENCE.

"See what you did. You know better than that."

"Don't pull the dog's tail. How would you feel if someone
pulled your tail?"[17]

The intuition of general principles is permanent, unchangeable, and ineradicable. This doesn't mean we can't twist or distort
it. To see how this works, let's recycle an example from a previous
chapter. The wrong of stealing from our neighbors is part of deep
conscience; it's one of the things I can't not know. On the other
hand, I may tell myself that taking from a rich man isn't stealing,
because he shouldn't have more than I have in the first place. *He's*
the real thief; I'm just rectifying the balance. Notice that even this
bit of rationalization draws upon real moral principles—equals

---

17. For these observations I am indebted to Ralph McInerny.

should be treated equally, wrongs should be set right—but by viewing them in a false light, it uses them to beat down another moral principle. Conscience is so deep that we are forced to use our moral knowledge (dishonestly) in order to suppress it. Notice that I said "suppress," not "erase."

In his letter to the Romans, Paul draws attention *both* to the witness of deep conscience *and* to its conflict with the distorted rationalizations of surface conscience:

> When Gentiles who have not the law do by nature
> what the law requires, they are a law to themselves,
> even though they do not have the law. They show that
> what the law requires is written on their hearts, while
> their conscience also bears witness and their conflict-
> ing thoughts accuse or perhaps excuse them[.][18]

The Bible presupposes deep conscience even where it does not mention it explicitly. A few examples will suffice. When God announces His intention to destroy the Cities of the Plain, Abraham protests in the name of God's own justice:

> Far be it from thee to do such a thing, to slay the
> righteous with the wicked, so that the righteous fare as
> the wicked! Far be that from thee! Shall not the Judge
> of all the earth do right?"[19]

In the prologue to the Ten Commandments, God reminds the people of their indebtedness to Him:

> And God spoke all these words, saying, "I am the LORD
> your God, who brought you out of the land of Egypt,
> out of the house of bondage. You shall have no other
> gods before me...[20]

---

18. Romans 2:14-15 (RSV).
19. Genesis 18:23-25 (RSV).
20. Exodus 20:1-3 (RSV).

In the letter to the Romans, Paul declares that not only the covenant people but the gentiles will suffer God's punishment for their sins:

> For God shows no partiality. All who have sinned without the law will also perish without the law, and all who have sinned under the law will be judged by the law.[21]

How is it that Abraham knows something about God's justice before the law of Moses? How is it that the Hebrews, to whom God is about to announce the Commandments, already know the law of gratitude? How is it that the gentiles, who have never heard of Torah, are accountable to God for their misdeeds? The answer is in all three cases the same: The basics of His law are already impressed upon the innermost design of the created moral intellect. We know a part of God's will for us through deep conscience, even before receiving it in words.

The Witness of Designedness in General

We think of pagans as people who don't know about the one God. Paul sees the matter differently. They aren't ignorant, but in denial:

> For the wrath of God is revealed from heaven against all ungodliness and wickedness of men who by their wickedness suppress the truth. For what can be known about God is plain to them, because God has shown it to them. Ever since the creation of the world his invisible nature, namely, his eternal power and deity, has been clearly perceived in the things that have been made. So they are without excuse[.][22]

The glory of God is proclaimed in the design of the microcosm:

---

21. Romans 2:11-12 (RSV).
22. Romans 1:18-20 (RSV).

For thou didst form my inward parts, thou didst knit
me together in my mother's womb. I praise thee, for
thou art fearful and wonderful. Wonderful are thy
works! Thou knowest me right well[.][23]

And it is proclaimed in the design of the macrocosm:

The heavens are telling the glory of God; and the fir-
mament proclaims his handiwork. Day to day pours
forth speech, and night to night declares knowledge.
There is no speech, nor are there words; their voice is
not heard; yet their voice goes out through all the
earth, and their words to the end of the world.[24]

It is proclaimed in the design of His providence:

In past generations he allowed all the nations to walk
in their own ways; yet he did not leave himself without
witness, for he did good and gave you from heaven
rains and fruitful seasons, satisfying your hearts with
food and gladness.[25]

It is even proclaimed in the design of their longings, for "He has
also set eternity in the hearts of men[.]"[26] To every desire there
corresponds some possible satisfaction: For hunger, food, for
wonder, knowledge, and so on. Yet there arise in us longings
which no natural experience can appease. It is as though we
were intended to surmise that mere nature is not the final word,
and to seek the Word behind it.

As to the design of the microcosm, it might be objected that
the microcosm merely appears to be designed, and that science

23. Psalm 139:13-14 (RSV).
24. Psalm 19:1-4 (RSV).
25. Acts 14:16-17 (RSV).
26. Ecclesiastes 3:11 (NIV).

has explained that appearance away. Science has not explained it away; dogmatic materialists wave it away. Mere intricacy might have come about one minute step at a time through random variation and natural selection, but the living cell turns out to contain myriads of molecular-scale machines, the distinctive feature of which is that all of their parts have to be present *at once* in order to work. According to Darwin, that is exactly the sort of datum that would decisively refute his theory.[27]

As to the design of the macrocosm, it might be objected that the macrocosm is not designed, but only beautiful. That raises the interesting question how *beauty* can be explained on materialist assumptions, but there is an even more telling point. Physicists have learned that if certain physical values did not happen to lie within an extremely narrow range, the universe would be inhospitable to biological life. Consider for example those heavens of which the psalmist speaks so eloquently. If the gravitational constant were minutely stronger than it is, stars would burn up too quickly. If it were minutely weaker than it is, they would never be able to ignite. The universe seems to have been fine-tuned for the possibility of life like us. "Fine-tuned," of course, is another word for "designed."

As to the design of God's providence, it might be objected that although our souls are gladdened by rains and fruitful seasons, they are also cast down by earthquakes and typhoons. If we are honest, we will admit that there is a mystery here. If we are *thoroughly* honest, however, we will admit that the goodness of life as such impresses us far more deeply than the evils that are incidental to it. Even Nietzsche, the author of the slogan "God is dead," admitted that at times he was overcome with gratitude. Gratitude to whom?

Finally, as to the design of our longings, it might be objected that the argument begs the question. According to the objector,

---

27. "If it could be demonstrated that any complex organ existed which could not possibly have been formed by numerous, successive, slight modifications, my theory would absolutely break down." Charles Darwin, *The Origin of Species*, 6th ed. (New York: New York University Press, 1988, orig. 1872), Chapter 6, at p. 154.

the premise that desires correspond to satisfactions does not prove design, but presupposes it. On the contrary, even the Darwinist concedes the correspondence of desires to satisfactions, but no desire would have evolved unless it had value for the organism. The problem the Darwinist faces is that on his assumptions, the things that satisfy our various desires must be available *in this world.* What then are we to make of the longing for "that unnameable something, desire for which pierces us like a rapier at the smell of a bonfire, the sound of wild ducks flying overhead, the title of *The Well at the World's End,* the opening lines of *Kubla Khan,* the morning cobwebs in late summer, or the noise of falling waves"?[28]

But what has the witness of the designedness of things in general to do with *moral* knowledge? Quite a lot. By pointing to the Designer, it tells us that we are not made for ourselves alone; we are answerable to Him. Moreover, if the Designer is real, then deep conscience, being part of the design, can be trusted; otherwise we might have mistaken it for mere evolutionary detritus, a leftover from the paleolithic past, something we should try to rise above.[29] Finally, the designedness of things in general directs our attention to the other features of our design, to which we turn next.

The Witness of the Details of Our Design

Designedness is important not only in general but in particular, for some of the Designer's intentions for us are plain from our blueprint—from the physical, emotional, intellectual, and

---

28. The quotation is from C.S. Lewis, whose discussion of this longing is exceptionally illuminating. See *The Pilgrim's Regress,* preface to 3d ed., p. xii.

29. Don't laugh; this is exactly how convicted murderer George E. Delury dismissed his pangs of remorse after poisoning and suffocating his wife. "It was not a moral guilt, an awareness of having done something ethically wrong; it was more immediate than that, almost physical.... I have come to believe we humans, like other primates, have an instinctual block against killing our own kind, a prohibition that, if violated, sets up strong undercurrents of dissonance.... It was this sort of primordial, instinctual unease that I felt and called 'guilt.'" George E. DeLury, *But What If She Wants to Die? A Husband's Diary* (Secaucus, N.J.: Birch Lane Press/Carol Publishing Group, 1997), pp. 178-179.

spiritual particulars of the *human* design. For illustration, consider just the most conspicuous feature of our design, the complementarity of the sexes. As Peter Motteaux wrote in the seventeenth century, with music by the great Purcell, "Man is for the woman made, and the woman for the man." A measure of our contemporary confusion is that we are less likely to be scandalized by his slightly ribald lyrics than by his theme.

Man, man, man is for the woman made,
And the woman for the man;
As the spur is for the jade,
As the scabbard for the blade,
As for digging is the spade,
As for liquor is the can,
So man, man, man is for the woman made,
And the woman for the man.[30]

Why make such a fuss about the complementarity of the sexes—why is it so important? In man as in other species, the purpose of the sexual powers is procreation. However, we aren't designed like guppies, who cooperate only for a moment. Among us, procreation requires an enduring partnership between two different kinds of humanity, mother and father, husband and wife, who are jointly irreplaceable because their differences correspond. These differences go all the way down and all the way up; they are not only biological, requiring dissimilar bodies to unite as a single organism, but spiritual, requiring the mutual and total gift of self. The spouses collaborate at every phase: At the point of conception, in that each provides a different gamete; in gestation and childhood, in that she

---

30. First of three stanzas, "Man Is For the Woman Made," Z. 605 no. 3, from *Deliciae Musicae*, Vol. III (1696); lyrics by Peter Motteaux, music by Henry Purcell. Notice the balance of the lyrics; man is for the woman made, *and* the woman for the man. Plainly one or the other is being teased in some of the analogies, but it is not always clear which one, and both sexes come in for their share.

protects the child and he protects them both; still later, in that the child needs two distinct models, one of each sex, as well as a model of their partnership. When at last the child is grown and the age of conception is past, even then the partnership lives on, for as the child establishes his own new family, he relies on their experience and counsel; procreation is thus a lifelong affair. This is the natural pattern of human generation. To ignore it is to set aside powers so august that it is easy to see how the pagans mistook them for gods.

We learn from Paul that the stakes are higher still. In a pointed remark about the rejection of God by the gentiles, he contrasts conduct that honors our species design with conduct that desecrates it:

> For this reason God gave them up to dishonorable passions. Their women exchanged natural relations for unnatural, and the men likewise gave up natural relations with women and were consumed with passion for one another, men committing shameless acts with men and receiving in their own persons the due penalty for their error.[31]

What Paul is talking about is not hard to fathom. Genesis had declared that man and woman *together* image God, not man alone, nor woman alone.[32] Sexual complementarity is therefore so fundamental to the *imago Dei* that one of the first effects of alienation between man and God is alienation between men and women. Moreover this is a *natural* consequence—God "gave them up" to dishonorable passions, meaning that He did not intervene to prevent nature from taking its course.

That last point can be generalized. Let's see how.

---

31. Romans 1:26-27 (RSV), emphasis added.
32. "So God created man in His own image, in the image of God He created him; male and female He created them." Genesis 1:27 (RSV).

The Witness of Natural Consequences

Borrowing from a succinct formulation in Paul's letter to the Galatians, another name for this final witness might be the law of the harvest:

Do not be deceived; God is not mocked, for whatever a man sows, that he will also reap.[33]

The Old Testament teaches the same lesson:

A wicked man earns deceptive wages, but one who sows righteousness gets a sure reward. He who is steadfast in righteousness will live, but he who pursues evil will die.[34]

Many read these words solely as a warning of eternal punishments, reserved for the life to come. That seems highly unlikely; as we know from everyday observation, many of wrongdoing's penalties kick in during the present life. He who cheats his friends loses them; he who indulges in heroin becomes its slave; we now know that he who makes his living by abortion meets his victims later in his dreams. Lives that go with the grain of the created universe tend to prosper; lives that go against it suffer loss, usually even by their own reckoning of "loss."

To be sure, in this life the law of the harvest does not work with perfect efficiency. Bad things do happen to good people, and vice versa. From special revelation, we learn that God's providence has taken this into account.[35] All things considered, however, it is astonishing just how efficient the law really is. Human history is largely the chronicle of spectacular failure to

---

33. Galatians 6:7 (RSV).
34. Proverbs 11:18-19 (RSV).
35. "We know that in everything God works for good with those who love him, who are called according to his purpose" (Romans 8:28, RSV).

outwit the witness of natural consequences. Those who wish to commit crimes with impunity become tyrants, only to discover that to maintain themselves in power they must commit even greater crimes than they had intended. Those who wish to unhook sex from procreation promote pills and prophylactics, only to discover that they have made out-of-wedlock pregnancy more common than before.

The psalmist wonders why the nations rage and the peoples plot futile things.[36] One suspects that they rage *because* they have plotted futile things: Their effort to escape natural consequences has its own natural consequences. It may change the form of the consequences, perhaps into something worse. It may deflect consequences onto others, perhaps our children or our children's children. What it cannot do is make them go away. So it is that the witness of natural consequences becomes the witness of last resort, the one which forces itself upon us when we have refused to listen to the other three.

General Revelation in Rabbinical Tradition

Considering the many allusions to general revelation not only in the New Testament but in the Old Testament, one would expect the natural law to be recognized not only by Christians but also by Jews. Why isn't is? Actually, it is. Although it is widely held that Judaism has no tradition of the natural law, it would be more accurate to say that Judaism does not use the *term* "natural law."

Modern Judaism approaches Holy Scripture through the prism of centuries of rabbinical reflection during which Talmud was laboriously written and expanded. This requires explanation. According to Judaism, the Torah or law of God has two parts, written Torah and oral Torah. Written Torah is contained in the first five books of the Bible. Though perfect, it is incomplete; it requires explanation, as well as principles of interpretation by which it can be applied to new circumstances. These

---

36. Psalm 2:1; see also v. 3. Translations vary.

explanations and principles are oral Torah, because after Moses it was transmitted down the centuries from teacher to teacher by word of mouth. Several hundred years after Christ, the kernel of oral law was itself set to writing. Because, in the principles of interpretation, it contained tools for its own elaboration, this writing was capable of voluminous expansion in later centuries. And because, as also mentioned, the principles of interpretation were believed to have been given by God, the vast literature that resulted was considered just as truly a part of God's revelation as Torah was. The resulting body of Jewish legal traditions is called *halakhah*, and the classical rabbinical commentary on these traditions is what we know as Talmud.

Talmudic learning has influenced the natural law tradition in at least two important ways. One very old rabbinical tradition is speculation about "the reasons of the commandments," that is, about the deeper purposes God may have had in giving the Hebrew people the ordinances of the Torah, or Law of Moses. Although some of His purposes transcend our finite powers of understanding, others are accessible through rational reflection. If this were not so, the rabbis reasoned, then Torah would have been unintelligible; rather than seeming good and righteous, it would have seemed arbitrary. Insofar as Torah was originally a civil code for the Hebrew people, the rabbinical distinction between the positive laws contained in Torah and God's reasons for giving them *parallels* natural law tradition's distinction between the positive laws made by governments and the moral principles, originating in God, from which they ought to be derived.

Another rabbinical tradition is the "seven laws given to the sons of Noah"—very general moral laws given by God to Noah and his "sons," or descendants, a group which of course includes every subsequent generation of human beings. The story of the rescue of Noah from the Flood mentions only three such commandments: Not to eat meat that still contains its lifeblood (Genesis 9:4), not to shed the blood of man (Genesis 9:5-6), and the proper use of the sexual powers to procreate and fill the earth (Genesis 9:7). According to oral tradition, however, there were actually seven.

One of the Noahide commandments is positive: Provision must be made for the administration of public justice (this is usually taken to mean courts). The rest are negative: There must be no idolatry, no blasphemy, no sexual immorality, no bloodshed, no theft, and no eating of flesh torn from living animals. Some rabbis held that up to six of these commandments had previously been given to Adam; others disagreed. Either way, the point is clear: No people now can claim to be ignorant of them; no nation now can claim to be exempt.

In the Talmudic view, this gives the Noahide commandments special importance for understanding relations between Jews and gentiles: Only the Jews have received Torah, but even the gentiles have received the Noahide laws. God does not require gentiles to follow Torah, but a gentile who lives up to the Noahide laws should be viewed differently than a gentile who does not.

5 | Natural Law in Western Law

Until recently, the Western legal tradition has self-consciously grounded itself on the natural law. Even today's jurists cannot quite shake off the idea of a higher law to which man-made law must conform, and which provides both the basis and the limits of its authority.

Let's take a look at some of the high points in the development of the neglected natural law foundations of our present-day law—Roman, English, and American.

The Natural Law in Roman Law

The natural law tradition has been powerfully influenced by the *Corpus Juris Civilis*,[37] a work commissioned in the sixth century A.D. by the Byzantine Emperor Justinian to harmonize a sprawling mass of legal material which had accumulated over a period of a thousand years—case law, enacted law, senatorial consults, judicial interpretations, and imperial decrees. Written under the supervision of Tribonius, the *Corpus* includes four parts: The *Codes*, a collection of imperial "constitutions" or legislation dating from the time of the Emperor Hadrian; the

---

37. *Corpus Juris Civilis*, meaning "body of civil law," is actually a modern name for the work, dating only to the sixteenth century.

Institutes, a manual for students of law; the *Digest*, or *Pandects*, a collection of excerpts from Ulpian, Gaius, and thirty-seven other great Roman jurists; and the *Novels*, added later, a collection of "new" legislation.

The noble aspiration of the *Institutes* is to ground the understanding of Roman law in fundamental moral principles:

> Justice is the constant and perpetual wish to render every one his due.
>
> Jurisprudence is the knowledge of things divine and human; the science of the just and the unjust....
>
> The maxims of law are these: to live honesty, to hurt no one, to give every one his due.[38]

The natural law features prominently in the discussion:

> The study of law is divided into two branches; that of public and that of private law. Public law regards the government of the Roman empire; private law, the interest of the individuals. We are now to treat of the latter, which is composed of three elements, and consists of precepts belonging to the natural law, to the law of nations, and to the civil law.[39]

Unfortunately, although the *Corpus Juris Civilis* played a great part in diffusing the concept of the natural law throughout the West, its understanding of the subject was not flawless, and it diffused both its insights and its confusions. One serious confusion is that what the *Institutes* call *just gentium*, the "law of

---

38. *Institutes*, 1.1.1-3, from *Medieval Sourcebook*,
    http://www.fordham.edu/halsall/basis/535institutes.html . Original source: Oliver J. Thatcher, ed., *The Library of Original Sources* (Milwaukee: University Research Extension Co., 1907), Vol. III: *The Roman World*, pp. 100-166.
39. *Institutes*, 1.1.4.

nations," is a more adequate natural law idea than what they call the "natural law." To see how so, let's consider each of these two concepts in turn.

Law of nations—not to be confused with international law—was a body of loose principles developed to provide for cases in which not all of the parties were Roman citizens. The reason it was called "law of nations" was that it drew from customs shared among many cultures and peoples. If you were to ask a Roman jurist *why* these customs were so widely shared, he would reply, following the jurist Gaius, that they were "decreed by natural reason," that they could be recognized as reasonable by common moral sense. According to this insight, if the law of nations is not identical with the natural law, it is at least closely related to it.[40] You can see the idea at work in the following passage of the *Institutes:*

> Civil law is thus distinguished from the law of nations. Every community governed by laws and customs uses partly its own law, partly laws common to all mankind. The law which a people makes for its own government belongs exclusively to that state and is called the civil law, as being the law of the particular state. But the law which natural reason appoints for all mankind obtains equally among all nations, because all nations make use of it. The people of Rome, then, are governed partly by their own laws, and partly by the laws which are common to all mankind.[41]

Unfortunately, when the *Institutes* got around to defining the natural law *as such*, they adopted Ulpian's characterization of the natural law as "what nature has taught all animals."[42] You can see this weaker idea at work in another passage of the *Institutes:*

40. *Digest*, 1.1.9.
41. *Institutes*, 1.2.1.
42. *Digest*, 1.1.1.3.

The law of nature is that law which nature teaches to
all animals. For this law does not belong exclusively to
the human race, but belongs to all animals, whether of
the earth, the air, or the water. Hence comes the union
of the male and female, which we term matrimony;
hence the procreation and bringing up of children. We
see, indeed, that all the other animals besides men are
considered as having knowledge of this law.

There is a grain of truth in Ulpian's definition; the natural law
is certainly *related* to natural instinct. The problem is that he
misunderstands the relationship, thinking that the natural law
and natural instinct are the same thing. This is impossible, for
law, among other things, is a reasonable command addressed to
a being with a mind who is capable of understanding what is
demanded. Viewing law this way, we can see that although animals are subject to natural instinct, only human beings are subject to the natural *law*. This difference between humans and
animals affects even the ways in we humans use the capacities
which we and the animals share. Both have powers of procreation, for example, but for us they are imbued with rational and
spiritual meaning the animals know nothing about; that is why
we have matrimony while they merely rut. To put it another
way, the so-called animal capacities of human beings are not the
same as the capacities of animals—the relation is not one of
identity, but of analogy.

The misleading result of this odd pair of definitions, one
from Gaius and one from Ulpian, was that the *Corpus Juris
Civilis* assigned to the law of nations the rational attributes of
the natural law, but assigned to the natural law only the sub-
rational attributes of instinct. Until this confusion was cleared
up in the thirteenth century, it terribly confused the counsels of
Western law. Such is the brutalizing tendency of our own secular culture that on the rare occasions when the natural law is
mentioned in law schools at all, the definition of Ulpian might
be quoted, but the conversation goes no further.

The Natural Law in English Law

English reflection on the natural law is a wide river. We have time to glance at only two of its tributaries, Henry de Bracton, who wrote around 1256, and William Blackstone, whose most important work was composed between 1765 and 1769.

Bracton's great work is *De Legibus Et Consuetudinibus Angliae* ("On the Laws and Customs of England"). When his subject permits, Bracton follows the *Corpus Juris Civilis* so closely that at times he is virtually quoting:

> The *praecepta iuris* are three: to live virtuously, to injure no one, to give to each man his right....
>
> Private law has a threefold division: it is deduced partly from the rules of natural law, partly from those of the *jus gentium* and partly from those of the civil law.[43]

Yet Bracton is not a mere secretary; he adds to, modifies, and strengthens the tradition that he has received. Case in point: The aspiration of natural law theory is not to abolish the common moral sense of plain people but to purify and elevate it. From this point of view, it is the great good fortune of English history that insight has flowed upward into law from the customs of the people, rather than downward from the inventions of isolated minds. Had it not been for Bracton, this history might not have been so fortunate. At the very beginning he insists that law is no less law for being unwritten:

> Though in almost all lands use is made of the *leges* and the *jus scriptum*, England alone uses unwritten law and custom. There law derives from nothing written [but] from what usage has approved. Nevertheless, it will

---

43. Henry de Bracton, *De Legibus Et Consuetudinibus Angliae*, Volume 2, pp. 25-26. From *Bracton Online*, http://hlsl.law.harvard.edu/bracton/Common. English translation Copyright (c) 1968-1977 by the President and Fellows of Harvard College.

not be absurd to call English laws *leges,* though they
are unwritten, since whatever has been rightly decided
and approved with the counsel and consent of the
magnates and the general agreement of the *res publica*
[commonwealth], the authority of the king or prince
having first been added thereto, has the force of law.[44]

Bracton's acuity is also demonstrated in the ways that he
deals with the shortcoming of the *Corpus Juris Civilis.* For example, he realizes that there is something missing in Ulpian's con-
flation of the natural law with natural instinct, yet on the other
hand he recognizes that the two things must be somehow
related. His solution to the puzzle is to distinguish between
instinct *as such,* and that which God intended to teach by pro-
viding us with instinct. For example, mere sexual attraction per-
tains to the natural law in the first sense, but marriage and
family pertain to it in the second. Here is his own explanation

Natural law is defined in many ways. It may first be said
to denote a certain instinctive impulse arising out of ani-
mate nature by which individual living things are led to
act in certain ways. Hence it is thus defined: Natural law
is that which nature, that is, God himself, taught all living things.... On the other hand,... the definition will
be this: Natural law is *that taught* all living things by
nature, that is, by natural instinct.... This is what is
meant when we say that our first instinctive impulses are
not under our control, but our second impulses are....
There are some who say that neither will nor impulse
may be called *jus, jus naturale* or *jus gentium,* for they
exist in [the realm of] fact; will or impulse are the means
by which natural law or justice disclose or manifest their
effect, for virtues and *jura* exist in the soul.[45]

---

44. Ibid., p. 19.
45. Ibid., pp. 26-27. Emphasis added.

Another difficulty with Roman jurisprudence was that it had never been able to give a coherent account of bondservice. It seemed to belong to the law of nations, for there were slaves everywhere. On the other hand it seemed to violate the natural law, for by nature, humans are persons, not things—*whos*, not *whats*. A completely adequate solution to this problem would require distinguishing between two different senses of the law of nations: That which is common to all nations *simply*, and that which is common to all nations *because of the natural law*. To put this another way, there are two things found everywhere among fallen men, not only the law written on the heart, but also the desire to evade it. For this reason, careful investigation is required to know whether a particular custom which happens to be found everywhere arises from the first universal or the second. Bracton does not go so far as to say all that, but in his cautious way he goes quite far:

> Manumission is the giving of liberty, that is, the *revelation* of liberty, according to some, for liberty, which proceeds from the law of nature, cannot be taken away by the *jus gentium* but only obscured by it, for natural rights are immutable. But say that he who manumits does properly give liberty, though he does not give his own but another's, for one may give what he does not have, as is apparent in the case of a creditor, who constitutes a usufruct in his property. For natural rights are said to be immutable because they cannot be abrogated or taken away completely, though they may be restricted or diminished in kind or in part.[46]

We must not leave Bracton without honoring his insistence on the rule of law *as such*. Even while denying that an English king has any constitutional superior, he insists that the king is

---

46. Ibid., pp. 27-28; emphasis added.

subordinate to the constitution itself, for it is law that makes rulers, not rulers the law. His own words are better:

> The king must not be under man but under God and under the law, because law makes the king, for there is no *rex* where will rules rather than *lex*.[47]

We need this reminder, for there will always be those who confuse their own wills with higher law. In Bracton's day they were kings; in revolutionary France they were "the people," or those who claimed to speak for them; in contemporary Europe they are international civil servants; in America they are imperious judges. In any given nation, at any given time, any group may entertain such a fantasy, whether a majority or a minority, for the question is not size, but presumption. Bracton will have none of this presumption. Authority *descends* to human beings; they do not originate it.

The other English thinker we consider is William Blackstone. His *Commentaries on the Laws of England* were the deepest and broadest channel through which English reflection on the natural law reached America, and they are worth quoting here at some length:

> Man, considered as a creature, must necessarily be subject to the laws of his creator, for he is entirely a dependent being....

> This will of his maker is called the law of nature. For as God, when he created matter, and endued it with a principle of mobility, established certain rules for the perpetual direction of that motion; so, when he created man, and endued him with freewill to conduct himself in all parts of life, he laid down certain immutable laws of

---

47. Ibid., p. 33.

human nature, whereby that freewill is in some degree
regulated and restrained, and gave him also the faculty
of reason to discover the purport of those laws....

Such among others are these principles: that we
should live honestly, should hurt nobody, and should
render to every one his due; to which three general
precepts Justinian has reduced the whole doctrine of
law....

This law of nature, being coeval with mankind and
dictated by God himself, is of course superior in obligation to any other—It is binding over all the globe in
all countries, and at all times; no human laws are of
any validity, if contrary to this: and such of them as
are valid derive all their force, and all their authority,
mediately or immediately, from this original.

But in order to apply this to the particular exigencies
of each individual, it is still necessary to have recourse
to reason.... And if our reason were always, as in our
first ancestor before his transgression, clear and perfect, unruffled by passions, unclouded by prejudice,
unimpaired by disease or intemperance, the task
would be pleasant and easy; we should need no other
guide but this. But every man now finds the contrary
in his own experience; that his reason is corrupt, and
his understanding full of ignorance and error.

This has given manifold occasion for the benign inter-
position of divine providence; which, in compassion to
the frailty, the imperfection, and the blindness of
human reason, has been pleased, at sundry times and
in diverse manners, to discover and enforce its laws by
an immediate and direct revelation....

Upon these two foundations, the law of nature and the law of revelation, depend all human laws; that is to say, no human laws should be suffered to contradict these.[48]

All this is very good, and Blackstone's devotion to the natural law deserves honor as well as emulation. The same cannot be said about every aspect of his theory of the natural law, and I have quoted selectively. His greatest weakness is an apparent voluntarism, a tendency in some places to place will over reason. We saw in chapter two that in its classical form, the natural law tradition understands genuine law as an ordinance of reason (rather than naked will), aimed at the common good (rather than special interest), made by public authority (rather than by private power),[49] and promulgated or made known (rather than kept secret). In Blackstone's definition of law, almost all of this drops out. Law is merely "a rule of action dictated by some superior being." By "superior" he means superior in power, God in the case of the natural law, the magistrate in the case of civil law. Unless Blackstone is expressing himself carelessly (which I do not believe), he is committing himself to the view that in order to be real law, a command need only be dictated by the one who has power over you—so that, although God's laws happen to be reasonable and good (and the magistrate's laws must conform to them), nevertheless they would not need to be either reasonable or good to be laws.

If Blackstone does mean what he says here, then he is caught in a false dichotomy which goes all the way back to Plato's

---

48. William Blackstone, *Commentaries on the Laws of England* (Oxford: Clarendon Press, 1765-1769), Volume 1, Introduction, Section 2. The Blackstone Core Curriculum series, to which *Natural Law for Lawyers* belongs, will also include a volume by Robert Stacey about Blackstone's influence on the American founding and American law.

49. Public authority may be exercised either by the whole community acting at once, or by magistrates who have care of the community. In custom, it is exercised by the whole community acting at once. This confirms Bracton's insight that unwritten law is real law; as Thomas Aquinas puts it in *Summa Theologica* I-II, Q. 97, Art. 3, where he considers the question, "custom has the force of a law, abolishes law, and is the interpreter of law."

Euthyphro. He seems to be suspended between two alternatives—either the natural law is good because God commands it (which makes goodness arbitrary), or God commands the natural law because it is good (which puts goodness above God Himself). Although in his definition of law he chooses the first alternative, in the following passage he tries to have it both ways:

> Considering the creator only as a being of infinite power, [God] was able unquestionably to have prescribed whatever laws he pleased to his creature, man, however unjust or severe. But as he is also a being of infinite wisdom, he has laid down only such laws as were founded in those relations of justice, that existed in the nature of things antecedent to any positive precept.

On the classical view, both alternatives are wrong, for they both assume that God and His goodness can be distinguished. The question then is only which one is higher. There is a third alternative. God simply *is* the good—Goodness Himself, in person. He is neither above it nor beneath it, because He is not distinct from it. To ask whether an unjust command of God would still be lawful doesn't even make sense, because if God could command injustice, He wouldn't be God. Omnipotence doesn't mean that He can will something contrary to His own being, that He can be other than Himself; what it means is that whatever He can will, He can do.

Since both sides agree that God's law is good, this discussion may seem to split hairs. Unfortunately, some hairs have to be split—not only for understanding God, but for understanding human affairs. For what are we to say when a government commands something evil? On the Blackstonian definition of law—a rule of action dictated by some superior being, meaning someone more powerful—an unjust law retains every bit of its lawfulness. But on the classical definition of law—an ordinance of reason, aimed at the common good, made by public authority, and promulgated—an unjust law is not really a law at all. It is a fraud, a deceit, a masquerade, and an act of force: Something called a law, that isn't one.

The Natural Law in American Law

The strongest testimony to the belief in the natural law at the beginning of the American republic comes not from our foundational legal document, the Constitution, but from our foundational political document, the Declaration of Independence. Following are its familiar opening words:

> WHEN in the Course of human Events, it becomes necessary for one People to dissolve the Political Bands which have connected them with another, and to assume among the Powers of the Earth, the separate and equal Station to which the Laws of Nature and of Nature's God entitle them, a decent Respect to the Opinions of Mankind requires that they should declare the causes which impel them to the Separation.

> WE hold these Truths to be self-evident, that all Men are created equal, that they are endowed by their Creator with certain unalienable Rights, that among these are Life, Liberty and the Pursuit of Happiness....

God is here presented as a Creator who has impressed certain laws onto His creation; the laws of nature are thus His laws, and their authority is His as well. Certain of these principles are called "self-evident," meaning that they are so plain to the mind that no one can honestly claim not to know them. One such principle is that all men are created equal, for if all men share the same nature and the same moral capacities, then no man can be the natural servant of another in the sense that a cow or a horse might be. From this fact follows *rights* of a sort that cannot be given up, cannot be taken away, and cannot be destroyed.

The words are Thomas Jefferson's, but the argument—here and elsewhere in the document—is John Locke's:

> [M]en being all the workmanship of one omnipotent, and infinitely wise maker; all the servants of one sovereign master, sent into the world by his order, and about his business; they are his property, whose workmanship they are, made to last during his, not one another's pleasure: and being furnished with like faculties, sharing all in one community of nature, there cannot be supposed any such subordination among us, that may authorize us to destroy one another, as if we were made for one another's uses, as the inferior ranks of creatures are for our's.[50]

Unlike the Declaration of Independence, the Constitution is strangely silent about the natural law. Very early in American history, two clashing schools of thought emerged, for although all early jurists believed in the natural law, they disagreed about whether judges may declare acts of the legislature void on grounds that they violate the natural law. This conflict appears in our case law as early as *Calder v. Bull* (1798), a case involving the meaning and validity of enactments *ex post facto*.[51] Justice Samuel Chase argues that judges *may* void legislative acts by direct appeal to the natural law, because if not, the legislature would be omnipotent:

> I cannot subscribe to the omnipotence of a State Legislature, or that it is absolute and without control; although its authority should not be expressly restrained by the Constitution, or fundamental law, of the State.... A few instances will suffice to explain what I mean. A law that punished a citizen for an innocent

---

50. John Locke, *Second Treatise of Government*, 2.6.
51. 3 U.S. 386 (Dall.) (1798).

action, or, in other words, for an act, which, when done, was in violation of no existing law; a law that destroys, or impairs, the lawful private contracts of citizens; a law that makes a man a Judge in his own cause; or a law that takes property from A. and gives it to B: It is against all reason and justice, for a people to entrust a Legislature with such powers; and, therefore, it cannot be presumed that they have done it. The genius, the nature, and the spirit, of our State Governments, amount to a prohibition of such acts of legislation; and the general principles of law and reason forbid them. The Legislature may enjoin, permit, forbid, and punish; they may declare new crimes; and establish rules of conduct for all its citizens in future cases; they may command what is right, and prohibit what is wrong; but they cannot change innocence into guilt; or punish innocence as a crime; or violate the right of an antecedent lawful private contract; or the right of private property. To maintain that our Federal, or State, Legislature possesses such powers, if they had not been expressly restrained; would, in my opinion, be a political heresy, altogether inadmissible in our free republican governments.

Justice Samuel Iredell maintains just as firmly that judges may *not* void legislative acts by direct appeal to the natural law, because if they could, then *they* would be omnipotent:

It is true, that some speculative jurists have held, that a legislative act against natural justice must, in itself, be void; but I cannot think that, under such a government, any Court of Justice would possess a power to declare it so. Sir William Blackstone, having put the strong case of an act of Parliament, which should authorise a man to try his own cause, explicitly adds, that even in that case, "there is no court that has power to defeat the intent of the Legislature, when couched in such evident and express words, as leave no doubt whether it was the intent of the Legislature, or no."⁵²

... If... the Legislature of the Union, or the Legislature of any member of the Union, shall pass a law, within the general scope of their constitutional power, the Court cannot pronounce it to be void, merely because it is, in their judgment, contrary to the principles of natural justice. The ideas of natural justice are regulated by no fixed standard: the ablest and the purest men have differed upon the subject; and all that the Court could properly say, in such an event, would be, that the Legislature (possessed of an equal right of opinion) had passed an act which, in the opinion of the judges, was inconsistent with the abstract principles of natural justice.

With variations, the opposing schools of thought represented by Chase and Iredell have persisted to the present day. It is crucial to understand the nature of the dispute. Chase and Iredell do *not* give different answers to the question "May judges void acts of the legislature on grounds that they violate the Constitution?" Both reply "Yes." Their dispute is about the natural law. They do *not* give different answers to the question "Is there a natural law?" Both reply "Yes." They do *not* give different answers to the question "Is it fitting for the legislature to enact a bill which violates the natural law?" Both reply "No." Their quarrel concerns a different question: "Who has the corrective authority to declare *when this has taken place?*" Chase replies, "The courts"; Iredell, "only the legislature itself." This is a question of prudence. The Constitution does not tell us which jurist is right, the natural law *as such* does not tell us which

52. Iredell is quoting from the *Commentaries on the Laws of England*, Introduction, Section 3, where Blackstone discusses principles of statutory construction.

jurist is right, and the dilemma is that tyranny seems to threaten no matter which way the question is answered.

This dilemma seems inescapable only because a crucial distinction has been missed by both sides. Natural law thinkers have always recognized a difference between the basic principles of the natural law and their remote implications. Chase seems to have in mind chiefly basic principles. These are known at some level to everyone, they require no great study to find out, and only obstinate minds could disagree about them. For this reason, Chase sees no reason why judges should not be able to say to misbehaving legislators, "You know better than that; your unjust act is void." By contrast, Iredell seems to have in mind chiefly the remote implications of basic principles. These are *not* necessarily known to everyone, they may require a great deal of study to find out, and even reasonable minds may disagree about them. Since legislators are not limited to the facts of the case at hand, as judges are, legislators have greater facilities for their investigation, so Iredell sees no reason why judges should be able to second-guess.

Each of the two antagonists, Chase and Iredell, makes good sense with respect to the kind of precept he chiefly has in mind. However, neither makes good sense with respect to the kind of precept the other chiefly has in mind. If I may propose a solution: In a system of divided government with checks and balances,

> 1. Courts *should* be granted authority to void legislative acts on grounds that they violate basic principles of the natural law such as "Do not murder" and "Punish only the guilty."

> 2. Courts should *not* be granted authority to void legislative acts when the only violations that are alleged concern remote implications of the basic principles.

I don't claim that this is an easy solution, only that it is a principled and prudent solution. No doubt it would take effort to draw the line well. One reason is that implications of basic principles may be more remote or less remote. Another is that human beings are capable of dispute even over the question of which things are reasonably indisputable. About the latter problem, I offer only one modest point: It does not follow that all things are reasonably disputable.

One more point, then we can close the chapter. Courts would not be able to avoid considerations of natural law even if they had *no* authority to void acts of the legislature. Considerations of natural law arise willy nilly, even in the mere interpretation of legislative acts whose validity is conceded. I owe my favorite illustration of this point to Professor Charles E. Rice. The 1932 *Restatement of Contracts* declares in Section 90.

A promise which the promisor should reasonably expect to induce action or forbearance of a definite and substantial character on the part of the promisee and which does induce such action or forbearance is binding if injustice can be avoided only by enforcement of the promise.

Put more simply, if breaking a contract would cause injustice, then the contract is binding. Now the *Restatement of Contracts* does not explain what "injustice" means; it expects readers to know that already. Suppose language like this were contained in statutory law. In such a case courts would be forced to work out *some* of the remote implications of the natural law, even if they were utterly deferential and their sole motive were to figure out what the statute meant by "injustice."

You may say that in such a case the legislature has legislated badly. It should not have used undefined terms like "injustice"; it should have defined them. But of course, nominal definition merely replaces a single word with a string of words, and the words in the string need definition too. For example, suppose you define injustice as the violation of justice; then you must define justice. Suppose you go on to define justice, à la *Corpus*

Juris Civilis, as "to live honesty, to hurt no one, to give every one his due"; then you must define living honestly, hurting no one, and giving every one his due. And so on.

You can replace many undefined terms by defined terms, but you cannot keep this up until nothing undefined is left. There will always be some rock-bottom undefined terms in terms of which the rest of the terms are defined—and some of those undefined terms will inevitably have moral meaning. This fact undermines all versions of legal positivism. It plagues not only the simple, "law is the command of the sovereign" versions, but also the more sophisticated "law is a convention" versions. It afflicts not only those versions which focus on ordinary legal rules, but also those versions which distinguish between these lower-level rules and other, higher-level rules by which the lower-level rules are established, recognized, or changed. No versions of legal positivism are exempt.

The moral of the story is that positive or man-made law points beyond itself; for much of its meaning, it inevitably depends on the natural law. I defy any legal positivist to show otherwise.[53]

---

53. Legal positivism also suffers from other problems which we have no space to discuss. For example, the version holding that law is the command of the sovereign suffers from circularity, because law is necessary to establish who the sovereign is; and the version holding that law is a social convention suffers from infinite regress, for it deems a law valid if it is conventionally *accepted as* valid. By substitution of terms, we find that it is valid if it is conventionally *accepted as* conventionally *accepted as* conventionally *accepted as*....

6 | The Classical Synthesis

In the natural law tradition, the classical synthesis was achieved by the thirteenth-century Dominican monk Thomas Aquinas, a thinker of unequalled depth and subtlety. Although St. Thomas supplements his biblical tools with various philosophical apparatus, especially from Aristotle, he reworks whatever he borrows; by the time he has finished reworking Aristotle, for example, the ancient Greek has transcended his pagan limitations. This is as we ought to expect. <u>Revelation transforms and illuminates reason</u>; it provides intellect with resources that it desperately needs but cannot provide for itself. *REVELATION AND REASON ILLUMINATE EACH OTHER*

St. Thomas's work is voluminous, but in a certain portion of his *Summa Theologica* commonly called the *Treatise on Law*[54] he gives a swift overview of what we may call the "architecture" of universal law—the way in which all of the kinds and dimensions of law fit together, beginning with their origin in God, reaching all the way down to man. This chapter gives an even swifter overview of St. Thomas's overview. You see in the diagram below a diamond shape, with the eternal law as the upper point of the diamond, the natural and the divine law as the left and

---

54. Comprising *Summa Theologica*, I-II, Questions 90-108. The abbreviation "I-II" means "First Part of the Second Part." Other abbreviations are also commonly used.

right points, respectively, and the human law as the lower point. I've drawn different kinds of arrows to indicate the different ways in which law flows down from God into man, and I'll explain these as I go along. Let's discuss each point of the diamond in turn. I will begin each section with a representative quotation from the *Treatise on Law*, then elaborate.

The classical synthesis is a resource for all Christians. It is drenched in the Holy Scriptures that God has given to the people of the covenant—yet it makes sense of that dim moral knowledge God has given to all men, even those outside of the covenant community.

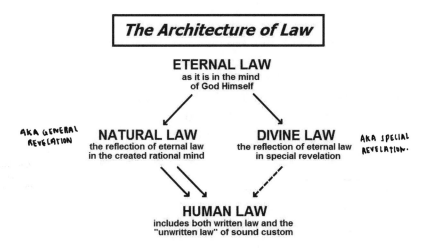

The Architecture of Law

ETERNAL LAW
as it is in the mind
of God Himself

AKA GENERAL
REVELATION   NATURAL LAW   DIVINE LAW   AKA SPECIAL
              the reflection of eternal law   the reflection of eternal law   REVELATION.
              in the created rational mind   in special revelation

HUMAN LAW
includes both written law and the
"unwritten law" of sound custom

Eternal Law

Now it is evident, granted that the world is ruled by
Divine Providence, that the whole community of the
universe is governed by Divine Reason. Wherefore the
very Idea of the government of things in God the
Ruler of the universe, has the nature of a law. And

since the Divine Reason's conception of things is not subject to time but is eternal, according to Proverbs 8:23, therefore it is that this kind of law must be called eternal.[55]

By the eternal law, we mean the principles by which God made and governs the universe—the pattern of His divine activity in creation and providence *as it is in the mind of God Himself.* This pattern is eternal because God is eternal. St. Thomas quotes from the great eighth chapter of the book of Proverbs to make his point, where Divine Wisdom declares "Ages ago I was set up, at the first, before the beginning of the earth."[56]

The fact that we call the pattern of this Wisdom *law* may seem problematic. Remember, one of the four conditions that must be satisfied for something to be real law is that it is promulgated or made known. It may seem that the eternal law is *not* made known because it exceeds the capacity of our finite minds. St. Thomas responds:

[N]o one can know the eternal law, as it is in itself, except the blessed[57] who see God in His Essence. But every rational creature knows it in its reflection, more or less.[58]

WE KNOW ETERNAL LAW THROUGH ETERNAL LAW'S REFLECTIONS, NATURAL LAW AND DIVINE LAW.

What is this "reflection" of the eternal law? In fact God has offered us two reflections, the natural and the divine law, to the first of which we now turn.

Natural Law

[T]he Psalmist after saying (Psalm 4:6): "Offer up the sacrifice of justice," as though someone asked what the works of justice are, adds: "Many say, Who showeth us

---

55. Thomas Aquinas, *Summa Theologica*, I-II, Question 91, Article 1.
56. Proverbs 8:23 (RSV).
57. The perfected souls in heaven.
58. Thomas Aquinas, *Summa Theologica*, I-II, Question 93, Article 2.

good things?" in answer to which question he says: "The light of Thy countenance, O Lord, is signed upon us": thus implying that the light of natural reason, whereby we discern what is good and what is evil, which is the function of the natural law, is nothing else than an imprint on us of the Divine light. It is therefore evident that the <u>natural law is nothing else than the rational creature's participation of the eternal law.</u>[59]

I remarked in the previous section that although we cannot know that unsearchable depths of the eternal law in itself, we can know it in its reflections. By the natural law, we mean its reflection in *general* revelation, especially in the deep structure of the created human intellect, which I have called deep conscience. This is the same thing Paul was speaking of when he referred to the law written on our hearts, in our inmost selves. The light of God's truth in our minds doesn't mean that we aren't sinful and in need of the grace of redemption. Nor does it mean that we know everything about right and wrong, that we require no instruction. But it is the foundation of everything we know about right and wrong, and the capacity that makes instruction possible. Without it, we could not even know that right and wrong are different.

To be sure, the eternal law is also reflected in other aspects of our design—such as the complementarity of male and female, and the system of natural consequences. But if it were not first reflected in the deep structure of the intellect, we would not be able to grasp the moral import of these other things. God's providence would guide us merely in the way that it guides the animals. Instead He has granted that it guide us in "the most excellent way":

Now among all others, the rational creature is subject to Divine providence in the most excellent way, in so far as it partakes of a share of providence, by being

59. Thomas Aquinas, *Summa Theologica*, I-II, Question 91, Article 2.

provident both for itself and for others. Wherefore it
has a share of the Eternal Reason, whereby it has a
natural inclination to its proper act and end: and this
participation of the eternal law in the rational creature
is called the natural law.[60]

God, so to speak, makes us *participants* in His Wisdom. This
is an incredible privilege. The animals are His pets, but we are
His children. Not only does He care for us, but He has endowed
us with the ability to understand in some measure the principles
of His care for us, and to care for each other in the same way.

By the way, it is for this reason, and this reason alone, that
the *human* law is possible. God could have arranged matters so
that we never had to deliberate about what is to be done, never
had to labor in order to grasp how the general principles of the
natural law should be applied to the particular circumstances of
our earthly communities. We may ask, "Why don't you make it
easier for us?" This is really like asking, "What is man that thou
art mindful of him, and the son of man that thou dost care for
him?"[61]—but in the mode of a complaint. The psalmist replies
that He has made us little lower than the angels, and has
crowned us with glory and honor. By creating us in His image,
by illuminating our intellects, by making us deliberating
beings, God draws us a little into His Wisdom, rather than
merely pushing us this way and that. All this, provided that we
cooperate.

St. Thomas explains that in a certain sense, all moral knowledge belongs to the natural law, but not all of it belongs to the
natural law in the same way. There are levels, or grades, of precepts. First level precepts are completely transparent; second
level precepts are only slightly less transparent; third level precepts are rather difficult. For this reason, he explains, second and
third level precepts are also promulgated in the Law of Moses:

60. Ibid.
61. Psalm 8:4 (RSV).

Now of these there are three grades: for some are most
certain, and so evident as to need no promulgation;
such as the commandments of the love of God and our
neighbor, and others like these,… which are, as it were,
the ends of the commandments; wherefore no man can
have an erroneous judgment about them. Some precepts are more detailed, the reason of which even an
uneducated man can easily grasp; and yet they need to
be promulgated, because human judgment, in a few
instances, happens to be led astray concerning them:
these are the precepts of the decalogue. Again, there
are some precepts the reason of which is not so evident
to everyone, but only the wise; these are moral precepts added to the decalogue, and given to the people
by God through Moses and Aaron.[62]

Unfortunately, St. Thomas's statement about judgment
being "led astray" concerning second level precepts is often misunderstood because of the obscurity of one of his examples, and
this is worth a brief digression. As he famously remarks in
another passage, "theft, although it is expressly contrary to the
natural law, was not considered wrong among the Germans."[63]
Many readers think he meant that human reason can be *totally
ignorant* of second level precepts such as the wrong of theft—
that the natural reason of all includes no more than the first
principle of practical reason, "good is to be done and pursued,

---

62. Thomas Aquinas, *Summa Theologica*, I-II, Question 100, Article 11. Compare
    Article 1: For there are certain things which the natural reason of every man, of
    its own accord and at once, judges to be done or not to be done: e.g. "Honor thy
    father and thy mother," and "Thou shalt not kill, Thou shalt not steal": and
    these belong to the law of nature absolutely. And there are certain things which,
    after a more careful consideration, wise men deem obligatory. Such belong to the
    law of nature, yet so that they need to be inculcated, the wiser teaching the less
    wise: e.g. "Rise up before the hoary head, and honor the person of the aged
    man," and the like. And there are some things, to judge of which, human reason
    needs Divine instruction, whereby we are taught about the things of God: e.g.
    "Thou shalt not make to thyself a graven thing, nor the likeness of anything;
    Thou shalt not take the name of the Lord thy God in vain."
63. Thomas Aquinas, *Summa Theologica*, I-II, Question 94, Article 4.

and evil avoided."[64] Not so. Not only was theft a punishable offense among the Germans, but St. Thomas was well aware of the fact. The source he cites is the sixth book of Julius Caesar's commentaries on the Gallic War. Caesar does not mention the routine Germanic penalties for theft, such as compensation. On the other hand, he says that the Germans considered such offenses so detestable that to propitiate their gods, they sought out thieves and robbers to be burned alive:

> [T]he men perish enveloped in the flames. They consider that the oblation of such as have been taken in theft, or in robbery, or any other offense, is more acceptable to the immortal gods; but when a supply of that class is wanting, they have recourse to the oblation of even the innocent.[65]

Has St. Thomas overlooked this passage? No, what he doubtless has in mind is a later passage where Caesar explains that the Germans approved stealing from tribes other than their own:

> Robberies which are committed beyond the boundaries of each state bear no infamy, and they avow that these are committed for the purpose of disciplining their youth and of preventing sloth.[66]

The manner in which the judgment of these barbarians was "led astray," then, is not that they were ignorant of the precept "Do not steal your neighbor's goods," but that they refused to recognize the members of other tribes as their neighbors. They didn't justify theft as such—just some theft. This is very much like the way the barbarians of our time make excuses for abortion.

---

64. Thomas Aquinas, *Summa Theologica*, I-II, Question 94, Article 2.
65. Julius Caesar, trans. W.A. McDevitte and W.S. Bohn, *The Gallic War*, 6.16. I am using the text webbed at the M.I.T. Internet Classics Archive, <http://classics.mit.edu>.
66. Ibid., 6.23.

"I know it's wrong to deliberately take innocent human life, but the fetus doesn't count as human life."

One point must be emphasized before closing this section: To say that the natural law is written on the heart of every human being is *not* to say that every human being is at peace with what is written there. For example, a human being may be drawn to something or take pleasure in something perverse, not because of created human nature, which is good, but because of a *corruption* of that nature in him. As St. Thomas explains:

> [I]t happens that something which is not natural to man, either in regard to reason, or in regard to the preservation of the body, becomes connatural to this individual man, on account of there being some corruption of nature in him. And this corruption may be either on the part of the body—from some ailment; thus to a man suffering from fever, sweet things seem bitter, and vice versa—or from an evil temperament; thus some take pleasure in eating earth and coals and the like; or on the part of the soul; thus from custom some take pleasure in cannibalism or in the unnatural intercourse of man and beast, or other such things, which are not in accord with human nature.[67]

Someone who does suffer such corruption will connaturally think and do and feel in a way which is radically contrary to his natural good, even to the point of considering his anti-good lovable:

> [W]henever [a man] uses [a] vicious habit he must needs sin through certain malice: because to anyone that has a habit, whatever is befitting to him in respect of that habit, has the aspect of something lovable, since

---

67. Thomas Aquinas, *Summa Theologica*, I-II, Question 31, Article 7.

it thereby becomes, in a way, connatural to him,
according as custom and habit are a second nature.[68]

.... in fact [the intemperate man] rejoices in having
sinned, because the sinful act has become connatural to
him by reason of his habit. Wherefore in reference to
such persons it is written (Proverbs 2:14) that "they are
glad when they have done evil, and rejoice in most
wicked things."[69]

It gets worse. Not only can a man come to love what is contrary to his connatural good—he can come to *hate* what *conduces*
to his connatural good. In other words, he can learn to loathe
those things which tend to the very happiness that he is naturally fashioned to seek. Evil of a particular kind will become second nature to him *even though it continues to be contrary to his
design*—but just because it *has* become second nature, he will
have difficulty recognizing it as evil:

Hatred of the evil that is contrary to one's natural
good, is the first of the soul's passions, even as love of
one's natural good is. But hatred of one's connatural
good cannot be first, but is something last, because
such like hatred is a proof of an already corrupted
nature, even as love of an extraneous good.[70]

The reality of the natural law does not make such things
impossible; it conditions the way they happen. We human beings
make use of our moral powers even when we do evil. The problem is that we make use of them in a perverse and distorted way.
Plainly, the natural law *by itself* is not enough. Reflection on the
need for something more leads us to the next point of the diamond.
We now end our digression, and pick up the thread again.

---

68. Thomas Aquinas, *Summa Theologica*, I-II, Question 78, Article 2.
69. Thomas Aquinas, *Summa Theologica*, II-II, Question 156, Article 3.
70. Thomas Aquinas, *Summa Theologica*, II-II, Question 34, Article 5.

Divine Law

Besides the natural and the human law it was necessary
for the directing of human conduct to have a Divine
law. And this for four reasons.[71]

As the natural law is the reflection of the eternal law in general revelation, so the divine law is the reflection of the eternal
law in special revelation—in how God has disclosed Himself to
the community of faith. The traditional language of "natural
law" and "divine law" is often misunderstood. Both are divine in
the sense that they come from God, but they come from Him
in different ways—one in the book of creation, the other, still
better, in the book of Holy Scripture. These two reflections
overlap, but as we saw in chapter two, each contains some things
the other does not. We need them both.

Since God has given us a reflection of His eternal law in the
natural law—and since we do work out its implications through
the shared work of the human law—it may not be obvious why
a divine law is needed at all. St. Thomas explains:

First, because it is by law that man is directed how to
perform his proper acts in view of his last end. And
indeed if man were ordained to no other end than that
which is proportionate to his natural faculty, there would
be no need for man to have any further direction of the
part of his reason, besides the natural law and human law
which is derived from it. But since man is ordained to an
end of eternal happiness which is inproportionate to
man's natural faculty... therefore it was necessary that,
besides the natural and the human law, man should be
directed to his end by a law given by God.[72]

By our "last end," St. Thomas means the ultimate purpose
for which we were made—the vision of God in glory. This is

---

71. Thomas Aquinas, *Summa Theologica* I-II, Question 94, Article 4.
72. *Summa Theologica*, I-II, Question 91, Article 4.

"inproportionate" to our natural abilities in the sense that we could never achieve it on our own; we need the grace of God. When St. Thomas says that we are instructed toward this grace by "law," he is not endorsing the attitude that we can "earn our way into heaven," for he knows that our salvation was purchased by the blood of Christ. As Paul explains, "For in Christ Jesus neither circumcision nor uncircumcision is of any avail, but faith working through love."[73] But if what Paul says is true, then the *ways* of faith working through love, and the *means of grace* by which it becomes possible for us to have that faith that works through love, must be revealed to us by God Himself. These ways and means are what St. Thomas calls the divine law.

> Secondly, because, on account of the uncertainty of human judgment, especially on contingent and particular matters, different people form different judgments on human acts; whence also different and contrary laws result. In order, therefore, that man may know without any doubt what he ought to do and what he ought to avoid, it was necessary for man to be directed in his proper acts by a law given by God, for it is certain that such a law cannot err.[74]

In speaking of the "uncertainty of human judgment," St. Thomas is not thinking of one person forming the judgment "Murder is wrong" and another forming the judgment "Murder is right." Thanks to the natural law, it is not about that sort of thing that we humans become confused. What trips us up are the details; proper application of the natural law to particular circumstances requires wisdom and careful reflection. The divine law does not answer every question about the details, but it provides help, and the help that it provides can be trusted absolutely.

---

73. Galatians 5:6 (RSV).
74. Thomas Aquinas, *Summa Theologica*, Question 91, Article 4.

Thirdly, because man can make laws in those matters
of which he is competent to judge. But man is not
competent to judge of interior movements, that are
hidden, but only of exterior acts which appear: and yet
for the perfection of virtue it is necessary for man to
conduct himself aright in both kinds of acts.
Consequently human law could not sufficiently curb
and direct interior acts; and it was necessary for this
purpose that a Divine law should supervene.[75]

(margin note: ③ NEED DIVINE LAW TO GOVERN THE INTERIOR ALSO, WHICH MAN CAN NOT SEE.)

The human law can meaningfully forbid acts against charity,
like murder, but it cannot meaningfully command the virtue of
charity; it can meaningfully forbid acts of covetousness, like theft,
but it cannot meaningfully forbid the vice of covetousness. The
reason is that only what I do with my body can be detected; the
movements of the heart from which these acts arise are invisible.
Suppose the legislature did try to command charity; how could
the authorities tell whether I was in compliance? The fact that I
am doing the right things outwardly isn't proof positive; I might
be faking. The divine law has no such limitation, because God's
vision penetrates the hidden recesses of my soul.

Fourthly, because, as Augustine says…, human law cannot punish or forbid all evil deeds: since while aiming at
doing away with all evils, it would do away with many
good things, and would hinder the advance of the common good, which is necessary for human intercourse. In
order, therefore, that no evil might remain unforbidden
and unpunished, it was necessary for the Divine law to
supervene, whereby all sins are forbidden.[76]

In fact St. Thomas gives two reasons why the human law
cannot forbid all evil deeds. The first is given in the passage just

---

75. Ibid.
76. Ibid.

quoted: If you indiscriminately pull up all the weeds, you may
uproot some shoots of wheat along with them. For instance, it
would be difficult to completely suppress greedy profiteering
without also interfering with honest efforts to make a living.
The second is given in another passage, where St. Thomas
explains that "laws imposed on men should also be in keeping
with their condition," leading them to virtue gradually rather IMPOSE
than all at once; imperfect men whose favorite vices have been VIRTUE GRADUALLY
forbidden will "break out into yet greater evils."[77] For instance,
if you forbid cigarettes, they may pop amphetamines instead, or
they may establish a black market in cigarettes, using their
inflated profits to corrupt the police.

Which human laws can be enacted without inadvertently
bringing about more evil than good? The answer varies with
circumstances and can be quite difficult to discern. But the
divine law is free from such handicaps, for God is a consuming
fire. His Word condemns *all* that hinders charity and destroys
His creatures.

Human Law

[I]t is from the precepts of the natural law, as from
general and indemonstrable principles, that the human HUMAN LAW
reason needs to proceed to the more particular deter- NECESSITY
mination of certain matters. These particular determinations, devised by human reason, are called human
laws, provided that the other essential conditions of
law be observed[.][78]

By the human law, we mean the application of the natural
law, by public authority, to the circumstances of particular
human societies. Those who apply it may not realize that this is
what they are doing, but to reason correctly from general considerations of what is good and right *is* to apply the natural law.

---

77. *Summa Theologica*, I-II, Question 96, Article 2.
78. Thomas Aquinas, *Summa Theologica*, I-II, Question 91, Article 3.

The human law depends on the natural law for its authority. If human legislators refuse to enact what is good and
right—for example if they twist their decrees in order to give
undeserved benefits to certain groups, or lay undeserved burdens on others—then insofar as these mandates deviate from
the natural law, they are not true laws, but frauds and acts of
violence. We saw in chapter two that St. Thomas considers the
circumstances under which civil disobedience might be justified, or even obligatory. In other works[79] he considers how to
keep rulers from becoming tyrannical in the first place, and
what to do about them if they have.

You may have noticed that in the diagram at the head of
this chapter, the arrows leading from the natural and the divine
law to the human law are different than the arrows leading to
the natural and the divine law from the eternal law. Single solid
arrows lead down from the eternal law to the natural and the
divine law, because both the natural and the divine law are
reflections of the eternal law. A pair of solid arrows runs from
the natural to the human law, showing that there are two different ways in which the human law can be grounded on the
natural law. A dashed arrow connects the divine with the
human law, because the relationship between the divine and the
human law is not one of coercive enforcement. These matters
remain to be explained.

First let us consider the relationship between the divine and
the human law. It would not do to connect these by means of a
solid arrow, because according to St. Thomas, the responsibility to enforce the divine law does not belong to government. To
be sure, government enforces those *parts* of the divine law that
are also included in the natural law, such as the prohibition of
murder. However, the parts of the divine law that are *not*
included in the natural law belong to the discipline of the
Church, not the State. The reason isn't that these are less
important, but that God has ordained different institutions to

PARTS OF
DIVINE LAW
THAT ARE
INCLUDED
IN NATURAL
CAN BE
ENFORCED
HOWEVER.

---

79. Especially *De Monarchia* ("On Kingship").

do different things. The mission of the State concerns the proximate and temporal purposes of human life, whereas the mission of the Church concerns the ultimate and eternal purposes of human life. Besides, like hope and love, faith is not of such a nature that it can be compelled. In chapter one I quoted the remark of St. Hilary of Poitiers, "God does not want unwilling worship, nor does He require a forced repentance." St. Thomas agrees.

DIFFERENCES IN MISSION OF THE CHURCH AND THE STATE.

But in this case why is *any* line drawn between the divine and the human law? Instead of a dashed line, why not no line at all? Because although the State should not *enforce* those matters that come under the discipline of the Church, it should certainly be friendly and cooperative about them. So there is a relationship between the divine and the human law, but it is a relationship of honor, not enforcement.

The relationship between the natural and the human law does involve enforcement; that which the natural law prohibits should be prohibited by the human law as well, within the limits of prudence already mentioned. But I said above that there are two different ways in which the human law can be grounded on the natural law. What is all this about?

A pair of examples will make the matter clear. Example one: The natural law informs us that we should not gratuitously harm our neighbors. One way I might gratuitously harm my neighbor is to slip arsenic into his morning coffee. Such acts are wrong whether public authority takes note of them or not. However, public authority enacts a law declaring that such acts are punishable, and specifying what their punishment shall be. St. Thomas calls this way of grounding the human on the natural law "conclusion," short for "conclusion from premises."

DETERMINATION.

Example two: The natural law informs us that we should have regard for the safety of our neighbors. One threat to their safety is collision on the public roads. But the risk of collision might be minimized in many ways. For example, travelers might all drive on the right, or they might all drive on the left. These solutions are mutually exclusive; travelers cannot all drive on

CONCLUSION

the right *and* all drive on the left. Therefore, public authority simply chooses one of the solutions: "All vehicles shall drive on the right." St. Thomas calls this way of grounding the human on the natural law "determination." It differs from the other way, conclusion, because it requires choice among possible responses. Determination is also different from conclusion because it *makes* something wrong which was not previously wrong—in this case, driving on the left.[80]

Because the human law can be grounded on the natural law in two ways, conclusion or determination, there are also two *parts* of the human law, provisions that are derived by way of conclusion and provisions that are derived by way of determination. Provisions of the former kind are likely to be cultural universals—we will meet them in the legal cultures of all peoples in all times and places. Provisions of the latter kind are *not* likely to be cultural universals—they will vary widely among legal cultures. This at last makes sense of the ancient distinction between *jus gentium* and *jus civile*, the law of nations and the civil law.[81] It also helps us to reply to naive persons who say,

[margin note: CIVIL LAW VS. LAWS OF THE NATIONS]

---

80. Among other writers, William Blackstone also calls attention to the difference between conclusion and determination as ways of grounding human law in natural law: "There are, it is true a great number of indifferent points, in which both the divine law and the natural leave a man at his own liberty; but which are found necessary for the benefit of society to be restrained within certain limits. And herein it is that human laws have their greatest force and efficacy; for, with regard to such points as are not indifferent, human laws are only declaratory of, and act in subordination to, the former. To instance in the case of murder; this is expressly forbidden by the divine, and demonstrably by the natural law; and from these prohibitions arises the true unlawfulness of this crime. Those human laws that annex a punishment to it, do not at all increase its moral guilt, or superadd any fresh obligation *in foro conscientiae* to abstain from its perpetration. Nay, if any human law should allow or enjoin us to commit it, we are bound to transgress that human law, or else we must offend both the natural and the divine. But with regard to matters that are in themselves indifferent, and are not commanded or forbidden by those superior laws; such, for instance, as exporting of wool into foreign countries; here the inferior legislature has scope and opportunity to interpose, and to make that action unlawful which before was not so." Blackstone, *Commentaries on the Laws of England*, Introduction, 2.

81. In our own legal culture, both terms are now used in different senses. The expression "law of nations" is now usually confined in meaning to the natural law basis of international law, and the expression "civil law" is confined in meaning to that portion of a country's laws which deals with private rights and duties.

"If the natural law really existed, then everyone would have the same laws." No, because of sin; no, because of error; and no, because in a perfectly innocent way, what is derived from the natural law by way of determination may vary from place to place.

A Final Word about Custom

We've seen in previous chapters that sound custom is also a part of the human law, and the distinction we have been discussing applies to custom too. Sound customs arise as expressions of the judgment of the whole community as to how the common good shall be served. Although all such judgments are based tacitly on the natural law, they may express either conclusions or determinations of the natural law. For example, the custom of exchanging courtesies upon meeting expresses a conclusion; it eases social life everywhere. On the other hand, what counts as a courteous exchange may vary among cultures, and the fact that a particular culture deems *this* and not *that* in line with courtesy may express not a conclusion but a determination.

The custom of doing things one way rather than another is much like the choice of spouse. Let us suppose that Leah is just as virtuous and beautiful as Rachel, but Rachel is the one who Jacob loves. If he had simply chosen the more virtuous and beautiful sister over the less, then we would say that he had made a *prudential* determination. As I've set up the story, however, he has made a *free* determination. He has chosen Rachel for herself over Leah for herself—the goodness of *who-Rachel-is* over the equal but different goodness of *who-Leah-is*—not because Rachel is *more good in herself* than Leah but because she seems *more good to him*. Had Leah been his choice, it would have been no sin.

In the same way, the custom of our own land may be to meet each other's eyes as an expression of frankness, or cast them down as an expression of modesty; it may be to stand close to our friends to show intimacy, or at a slight distance to show respect; it may be to eat quietly because we are different from the animals, or belch loudly because we are grateful to our host. The collective judgment that our custom is *this* and not *that* may show that we think one good better than another; on the other hand, it may simply show which of various possible goods we have elected, in this custom, to express. Like different vocations, and different kinds of prayer, different customs and cultures may be said to specialize in different aspects of real good. The universal structures of morality are thus like the universal structures of music: Rather than making every song the same, they make possible an infinity of melodies.

7 | Debunking a Myth

During the modern period, the classical synthesis came unglued. Recovery began in the nineteenth century, and a renaissance of the natural law tradition is underway today. During the same period, the assault on the natural law has intensified. In the next chapter we will take a look at just a few of the forces in play. Before doing that, however, it's necessary to clear our minds of a great myth which has divided counsel and caused needless conflict among Christians.

It is commonly held that the Protestant Reformers rejected the natural law. They didn't. This fact is so important—yet so often denied by thinkers who consider themselves Reformed— that a departure from my usual procedure is demanded. I have tried not to overload readers with quotations in this book, but if I fail to document what the Reformers really believed, I risk the accusation of making it all up.

Martin Luther begins his thoughts about these matters with recognition that the pagans have a certain fragmentary knowledge of God Himself:

> Because of a natural instinct the heathen also have this
> understanding; they know that there is a supreme
> deity, that he must be worshiped, called upon, and

praised, and that one should take refuge with him in all dangers. Paul says that they have a natural knowledge of God (Rom. 1:21). For God has implanted this knowledge in the hearts of all human beings. They call God a helper, kind, and forgiving, even though afterwards they are in error as to who that God is and how He wants to be worshiped.[82]

His discussions of the natural law are characterized by an emphasis on the Golden Rule. Here is what he says in one of his sermons:

GOLDEN RULE - EVIDENCE OF THE NATURAL LAW
Not an individual is there who does not realize, and who is not forced to confess, the justice and truth of the natural law outlined in the command, "All things therefore whatsoever ye would that men should do unto you, even so do ye also unto them." The light of this law shines in the inborn reason of all men. Did they but regard it, what need have they of books, teachers or laws? They carry with them in the depths of their hearts a living book, fitted to teach them fully what to do and what to omit, what to accept and what to reject, and what decision to make.[83]

He makes the same point in *On Secular Authority:*

For nature teaches the same as love: I ought to do what I would have done unto me. And therefore I may not rob another, however good my claim, since I myself do not want to be robbed.... And this is how illgotten gains should be treated, whether they were

---

82. Martin Luther, *Luther's Works*, Volume 3, *Lectures on Genesis*, Chapters 15-20, remarks on Genesis 17:8 (Saint Louis: Concordia Publishing House).

83. Martin Luther, "Sermon for the Fourth Sunday after Epiphany: Romans 13:8-10," in *The Sermons of Martin Luther* (Grand Rapids: Baker Book House, 1983), Vol. 7, p. 73.

come by secretly or openly, so that love and natural
law will always prevail.[84]

But the Golden Rule is not the only precept written on
the heart. According to Luther, we also know naturally the Ten
Commandments:

> From this you perceive that the Creed is a doctrine
> quite different from the Ten Commandments; for the
> latter teaches indeed what we ought to do, but the
> former tells what God does for us and gives to us.
> Moreover, apart from this, the Ten Commandments
> are written in the hearts of all men[.][85]

Luther perceives clearly that if we did not have natural
knowledge of the basics of right and wrong, then God's teaching would make no sense to us:

> Experience itself shows that all nations share this com-
> mon ordinary knowledge.... I feel in my heart that I
> certainly ought to do these things for God, not because
> of what traditional written laws say, but because I
> brought these laws with me when I came into the
> world... For although the decalogue was given in one
> way at a single time and place, all nations recognize
> that there are sins and iniquities.[86]

Here he puts the point even more bluntly:

> [W]ere it not naturally written in the heart, one would
> have to teach and preach the law for a long time before

---

84. Martin Luther, *On Secular Authority*, in Harro Hopfl, *Luther and Calvin on
    Secular Authority* (Cambridge, England: Cambridge University Press, 1991).
85. Martin Luther, *Large Catechism*, 2.3. I am using the translation webbed at the
    Christian Classics Ethereal Library at www.ccel.org.
86. Quoted in Paul Althaus, *The Ethics of Martin Luther*, trans. Robert C. Schultz
    (Philadelphia: Fortress Press, 1972), pp. 26-28.

[margin note: BECAUSE WE KNOW RIGHT FROM WRONG, WE CAN TEACH AND TRAIN OURSELVES TO DO RIGHT, NOT WRONG.]

it became the concern of conscience. The heart must also find and feel the law in itself. Otherwise, it would not become a matter of conscience for anyone.[87]

John Calvin also acknowledges the natural knowledge of God. Here is what he says about it in his *Institutes of the Christian Religion:*

> That there exists in the human minds and indeed by natural instinct, some sense of Deity, we hold to be beyond dispute, since God himself, to prevent any man from pretending ignorance, has endued all men with some idea of his Godhead, the memory of which he constantly renews and occasionally enlarges, that all to a man being aware that there is a God, and that he is their Maker, may be condemned by their own conscience when they neither worship him nor consecrate their lives to his service.[88]

And again:

> All men of sound Judgment will therefore hold, that a sense of Deity is indelibly engraven on the human heart. And that this belief is naturally engendered in all, and thoroughly fixed as it were in our very bones, is strikingly attested by the contumacy of the wicked, who, though they struggle furiously, are unable to extricate themselves from the fear of God.... Whence we infer, that this is not a doctrine which is first learned at school, but one as to which every man is, from the womb, his own master; one which nature herself allows no individual to forget, though many, with all their might, strive to do so.[89]

---

87. Ibid.
88. John Calvin, *Institutes of the Christian Religion*, 1.3.1. For this and subsequent quotations from Calvin I am using the public-domain translations webbed at Christian Classics Ethereal Library, www.ccel.org.
89. Ibid., 1.3.2.

What about the natural law? Surprisingly, Calvin gives it even more attention than Luther does. Although he is often held to believe that fallen man's knowledge of natural law is negligible or nonexistent, that is simply not what he says. The import of the following passage from the *Institutes* is unmistakable:

If the Gentiles have the righteousness of the law naturally engraven on their minds, we certainly cannot say that they are altogether blind as to the rule of life. Nothing, indeed is more common, than for man to be sufficiently instructed in a right course of conduct by natural law, of which the Apostle here speaks.[90]

This is no fluke. He returns to the theme again:

[W]e observe that there exist in all men's minds universal impressions of a certain civic fair dealing and order. Hence, no man is to be found who does not understand that every sort of human organization must be regulated by laws, and who does not comprehend the principles of those laws. Hence arises that unvarying consent of the nations and of individual mortals with regard to laws. For their seeds have, without teacher or lawgiver, been implanted in all men.[91]

And again:

Now, as it is evident that the law of God which we call moral, is nothing else than the testimony of natural law, and of that conscience which God has engraven on the minds of men, the whole of this equity of which we now speak is prescribed in it. Hence it alone ought to

---

90. Ibid., 2.2.20, discussing Romans 2:14-15. For this and subsequent quotations from Calvin I am using the public-domain translations webbed at Christian Classics Ethereal Library, www.ccel.org.

91. Ibid., 2.2.13.

be the aim, the rule, and the end of all laws. Wherever
laws are formed after this rule, directed to this aim,
and restricted to this end, there is no reason why they
should be disapproved by us, however much they may
differ from the Jewish law, or from each other[.][92]

In case anyone should think that the grace of God somehow
supercedes the natural law, Calvin makes clear that this is not at
all the case. By the Gospel, the natural law is not abolished but
fulfilled—just what the classical synthesis maintained. Nor is he
patient with those who miss the point. In *On the Christian Life*,
he goes so far as to call denial of the natural law "monstrous":

[T]he duties of charity…. are not fulfilled by the mere
discharge of them, though none be omitted, unless it is
done from a pure feeling of love…. He who is thus
minded will go and give assistance to his brethren, and
not only not taint his acts with arrogance or upbraid-
ing but will neither look down upon the brother to
whom he does a kindness, as one who needed his help,
or keep him in subjection as under obligation to him,
just as we do not insult a diseased member when the
rest of the body labours for its recovery, nor think it
under special obligation to the other members, because
it has required more exertion than it has returned. A
communication of offices between members is not
regarded as at all gratuitous, but rather as the payment
of that which being due by the law of nature it were
monstrous to deny.[93]

As the following examples show, the same views are found
through his voluminous *Commentaries* on the Holy Scriptures.
As he remarks on Genesis 1:28:

---

92. Ibid., 4.20.16.
93. John Calvin, *On the Christian Life*, 2.

Now, what I have said concerning marriage must be
kept in mind; that God intends the human race to be
multiplied by generation indeed, but not, as in brute
animals, by promiscuous intercourse.... Still that
pure and lawful method of increase, which God
ordained from the beginning, remains firm; this is
that law of nature which common sense declares to
be inviolable.

On Genesis 41:38:

Pharaoh says nothing but what is naturally engraven
on the hearts of all men, that honors ought to be con-
ferred on none but competent persons, and such as
God has furnished with the necessary qualifications.

On Leviticus 19:32:

God teaches us that some sparks of His majesty shine
forth in old men, whereby they approach to the
honor of parents. It is not my purpose to gather quotations from profane authors in reference to the
honor due to the old; let it suffice that what God
here commands is dictated by nature itself. This
appeared at Athens, when an old man had come into
the theater, and found no place among his fellow-cit-
izens; but, when at length he was admitted with
honor by the Spartan ambassador, (because old age is
greatly reverenced among the Lacedemonians,)
applause was raised on all sides; and then the
Lacedemonian exclaimed, that "the Athenians knew
what was right, but would not do it." It was surely
manifested by this universal consent of the people
that it is a natural law in the hearts of all to reverence
and honor old men.

On Leviticus 18:6:

> In short, the prohibition of incests here set forth, is by
> no means of the number of those laws which are com-
> monly abrogated according to the circumstances of
> time and place, since it flows from the fountain of
> nature itself, and is founded on the general principle of
> all laws, which is perpetual and inviolable.... It may
> indeed be decreed that it should be lawful and unpun-
> ished, since it is in the power of princes to remit penal-
> ties; yet no legislator can effect that a thing, which
> nature pronounces to be vicious, should not be vicious;
> and, if tyrannical arrogance dares to attempt it, the
> light of nature will presently shine forth and prevail....
> Hence, just and reasonable men will acknowledge that,
> even amongst heathen nations, this Law was accounted
> indissoluble, as if implanted and engraved on the
> hearts of men. On this ground Paul, more severely to
> reprove the incest of a step-son with his father's wife,
> says, that such an occurrence "is not so much as named
> among the Gentiles."

On Isaiah 21:14:

> Yet as it is founded on the common law of nature and
> humanity, the Prophet indirectly insinuates that the
> hungry and thirsty are defrauded of their bread, when
> food is denied to them.

On Jeremiah 36:30:

> It seems then that it is to little purpose that the
> Prophet says, that his dead body would be exposed to
> the heat in the day, and to the cold at night. But this is
> to be referred to the common law of nature, of which
> we have spoken elsewhere[.]

On 2 Corinthians 12:14:

> Paul simply wished to show from the common law of nature, that what he had done proceeded from fatherly affection.

On Ephesians 5:31:

> A son is bound by an inviolable law of nature to perform his duties towards his father; and when the obligations of a husband towards his wife are declared to be stronger, their force is the better understood.

On Ephesians 6:1:

> Besides the law of nature, which is acknowledged by all nations, the obedience of children is enforced by the authority of God.

Just from these few quotations, we see that Calvin finds a natural law basis for the ordinance of marriage, the condemnation of fornication, the esteem due to the capable, the honor due to the old, the prohibition of incest, the help given to the needy, the affection of fathers for their children, the duties of sons toward their fathers (and more generally of children toward their parents), and the even greater duties of husbands toward their wives. These are not the words of someone who is hostile to the natural law.

Now that we have dispensed with the Great Myth, we are ready to consider how the classical synthesis came apart.

8 | What Happened?

What caused the classical synthesis to come apart? The answer is full of ironies. Some of the strongest solvents were applied by thinkers whose intention was to *affirm* the natural law as they understood it. Many attacks on the classical theory of the natural law confused it with mutated theories of the natural law introduced by thinkers who *also* rejected the classical theory. Christians have sometimes disparaged the natural law on the basis of assumptions they considered biblical but which they had actually absorbed from anti-Christian writers. A final oddity is that some arguments about the natural law are reactions against other arguments about the natural law—yet still oppose it.

Rather than reviewing the twists and turns of this complicated history, let us consider some of the more common arguments. Certain lines of attack appear over and over in the war against the natural law tradition.

The Argument from the Autonomy of Reason

A reiterated theme of the Enlightenment was that reasoning is reasonable only when it rejects all assistance from faith, limiting itself to resources it provides to itself. Although this argument does not oppose the natural law *as such*, it strongly opposes the classical synthesis. Formerly, God's revelations in the Bible and in creation had been thought to work together; the natural law was both presupposed by and illuminated by the divine, in that the divine law both alluded to and clarified the natural.[94] The Enlightenment philosophers who proposed the autonomy of reason rejected this balanced view. According to them, the natural law stands by itself, and divine law is superstitious nonsense.

Every powerful error gains its strength from the distortion or exaggeration of some truth. Those who believed in the autonomy of reason were certainly right to distinguish faith from reason. These really are different operations of the mind, and neither can force the other. In that important sense, reason is indeed autonomous. If this had been all they meant by speaking of the autonomy of reason, they would have been right. Unfortunately they meant nothing of the kind. They regarded faith and reason not just as different but as enemies, and they turned the idea that faith cannot force reason into the idea that reason cannot cooperate with faith. Crying "Reason Alone!", they never considered the possibility that faith might serve as an invitation to reason more fully and adequately.

This view of reasoning is itself quite unreasonable, for a certain kind of faith is necessary in order to reason at all. Suppose someone challenged a "Reason Alone" thinker to justify his confidence in reason. The only recourse available to him would be circular—he would have to reason about the matter. But circular arguments are themselves unreasonable; they cannot ground confidence in reason. What should we conclude from this fact? Not that our confidence in reason is misplaced, but that reason itself depends on a certain kind of faith. Nor is this the only way reason is faith-dependent. How do you know the moon isn't made of green cheese? You may say that the astronauts brought back rocks, but were you there? No, you have faith that expedition really happened and the rocks are what they say. Perhaps you add, "Yes, but in spectrographic analysis,

---

94. See chapters 2 and 3.

the light reflected from the moon differs from the light reflected from cheese." Very good, but have you conducted such tests yourself? Probably not, but you have faith in those who have. Even if you have personally conducted such tests, I might argue that the optical properties of cheese are different on the moon than they are on the earth. Perhaps you reply, "But the laws of physics are the same everywhere in the universe," and I agree with you. But have you checked everywhere in the universe to be sure? Of course not. You accept the uniformity and stability of the laws of the universe on faith.

If you protest that *these* sorts of faith are *reasonable* sorts of faith, I agree with you. But if some sorts of faith are reasonable, then isn't it also reasonable to ask whether faith in Christian revelation is one of the reasonable sorts? It is certainly reasonable *a priori*. If God wants us to know Him, if our unassisted powers are insufficient to know Him by ourselves, and if He is able to assist these powers by disclosing Himself more directly—then why wouldn't He? Faith in revelation is also reasonable *a posteriori*. In every case where the facts reported by the original witnesses can be checked, they turn out to have told the truth. Moreover, God's self-disclosure makes sense of many strange facts about reality that would otherwise remain unexplained. For example, try to find survival value in the capacity to be moved to awe by the beauty of the sunset; you will fail. Natural selection cannot account for it. The Christian revelation can. Such faith is a reasonable sort of faith.

By contrast, the faith expressed in the motto "Reason alone!" is *not* a reasonable sort of faith. Rather than considering whether Christian revelation might be reasonable, it obstinately refuses to look into the question at all. Rather than admitting that it too depends on a kind of faith, it witlessly claims that it doesn't. It assumes that we can know nothing important about God *except* that we can know nothing important about God, and refuses to justify this exception. It demands that we reason as though nature is all that there is, without giving any reason to believe that this is actually the case.

The Argument Against the Autonomy of Reason

Errors tend to come in pairs. If the Enlightenment ideologues exaggerated the autonomy of reason, some of their Christian critics have gone too far in the other direction. They have also confused the classical theory of the natural law with the debased theories promoted by the ideologues themselves. Consequently, viewing "natural law" and "autonomy of reason" as different names for the same thing, they have rejected them both. Here is a recent example:

> [T]he Achilles heel of natural law theory…. is that there is no body of truth or law existing apart from God's Word….
>
> [T]o the Rationalist mind, severed from the claims of Christ by the notion that natural law was accessible to reason, nothing could be more appropriate for ultimate allegiance than the rational analytical process itself, and of course this was soon seen in terms of scientific, empirical methods as the exploration of the physical world moved along….
>
> And natural law theory with its rationalism was the Trojan horse that brought the legions of Satan further and further into God's world.[95]

No one with the least knowledge of the natural law tradition could make such a sweeping claim. Far from suggesting that general and special revelation can contradict each other, the classical synthesis vigorously presented them as complementary. After all, both come from God; how could He contradict Himself? When a heterodox view called the "two truths" theory raised its head in

---

95. Rex Downie, "Natural Law and God's Law: An Antithesis." *The Christian Statesman* 42:1 (January-February, 1999); originally published in *The Christian Lawyer* 4:1 (Winter 1973).

the thirteenth century, suggesting that doctrines of the faith could somehow be true in theology but false in philosophy, the great natural lawyers Albertus Magnus and Thomas Aquinas exposed it as incoherent.[96] Along with the other architects of the classical synthesis, they viewed philosophy as the handmaid of theology: Not a slave, but a free and willing servant.

The Argument from the Inscrutability of Final Causes

According to this third criticism, no meaning or purpose is built into nature—or if any is, we cannot discover it. So far as *LIFE IS MEANINGLESS* we are concerned, it is intrinsically meaningless—merely stuff. *NATURE IS* The only purposes that count are *our* purposes, as we manipu- *PURPOSELESS* late it into doing what we want.

The originator of this argument was the sixteenth-century thinker Francis Bacon. According to the learning of his day, which followed Aristotle, to understand a thing is to know four things about it, called its "causes": Its material cause (what it is made of), efficient cause (what makes it happen), formal cause (form or essence), and final cause (the purpose for which it comes into being). Bacon did not deny that there are final causes. However, he insisted that the only final causes that we can actually know are the purposes that we ourselves bring to our productions:

> It is a correct position that "true knowledge is knowledge by causes." And causes again are not improperly distributed into four kinds; the material, the formal, the efficient, and the final. But of these the final cause rather corrupts than advances the sciences, except such as have to do with human action.[97]

---

96. The main champions of the "two truths" theory were Siger of Brabant and Boetius of Dacia. Thomas Aquinas attacked them in his works *De Unitate Intellectus Contra Averroistas* ("On the Unity of the Intellect Against the Averroists") and *De Aeternitate Mundi Contra Murmurantes* ("On the Eternity of the World Against the Whisperers").

97. Francis Bacon, *Novum Organum* ("The New Organon") 2.2

Since nature is not our production but God's, Bacon reasons, its purposes are inscrutable. Trying to find them out is a fool's errand, distracting us from real science:

> For the handling of final causes, mixed with the rest in physical inquiries, hath intercepted the severe and diligent inquiry of all real and physical causes, and given men the occasion to stay upon these satisfactory and specious causes, to the great arrest and prejudice of further discovery.[98]

Bacon's view has come to dominate science. On the face of it, however, it is absurd. Consider the body, for example. Are we really to believe that purposes of the eye, the heart, and the lungs are inscrutable? That they cannot be investigated? That the attempt to do so is a distraction and waste of time? Is it merely arbitrary to suggest that the first is for seeing, the second for pumping blood, and the third for taking in air? Your doctor would get a good laugh from that one. Nor is it only in biology that final causes can be studied, for language of purpose is at home whenever a part or aspect contributes in a systematic way to a greater whole. In fact, it is at home whenever you are forced to describe what something does in order to explain why it is the way it is. Consider for example a fact that has recently come to light in physics: The fundamental constants of the laws of physics (for example, the ratio of the nuclear energy levels of Carbon 12 and Oxygen 16) appear to be exquisitely fine-tuned for the *purpose* of making life like us possible—a point to which I alluded in chapter four. Were their values even minutely different than they are, we would not be here to talk about it. The Nobel Prize-winning astrophysicist Fred Hoyle, an atheist, was so stunned by such coincidences that he wrote, "A common sense interpretation of the facts suggests that a superintellect has monkeyed with physics,

ANTHROPIC
PRINCIPLE
FINE TUNING

---

98. Francis Bacon, *The Advancement of Learning*, 2.7.7.

as well as with chemistry and biology, and that there are no blind forces worth speaking about in nature."[99] Of course it would be unreasonable to expect Bacon to have known about nuclear energy levels, but he knew about eyes and hearts and lungs. The ease with which certain Christian writers fall in with the notion that God's creation has no meaning is quite amazing. "In a way," writes John W. Robbins, "we can be glad that nature teaches us nothing: If it did, we, like the Marquis de Sade, would learn all the wrong lessons."[100] In chapter three I commented on the gibe that natural law theory "baptizes Aristotle"; it would be more accurate to say that Robbins baptizes Enlightenment skepticism. As he writes admiringly of the Enlightenment paragon David Hume:

> Natural law is a failure, as David Hume so obligingly pointed out, because "oughts" cannot be derived from "ises." In more formal language, the conclusion of an argument can contain no terms that are not found in its premises. Natural lawyers, who begin their arguments with statements about man and the universe, statements in the indicative mood, cannot end their arguments with statements in the imperative mood.[101]

[handwritten margin note: WE CAN NOT LOOK AT WHAT IS AND ASSUME WHAT IT OUGHT TO DO, WHAT IT OUGHT TO BE.]

But Hume was mistaken; what a thing *is* and how it *ought* to be are closely connected. An *is* that just "happens to be" does not imply an *ought* because it is arbitrary; he was right about that. But an *is* that indicates purpose is fraught with an *ought* already. For example, an eye is a thing for seeing, a knife is a thing for cutting, and a man is a thing for imaging God; that is

99. Fred Hoyle, "The Universe: Past and Present Reflections," *Annual Review of Astronomy and Astrophysics* 20 (1982), pp. 1-35, at p. 16.
100. John W. Robbins, "Truth and Foreign Policy." The Trinity Foundation, March, 1991.
101. John W. Robbins, "An Introduction to Gordon H. Clark." *The Trinity Review* (July-August 1993).

what they *are.* Thus a good eye is an eye that sees well, a good knife is a knife that cuts well, and a good man is a man that images God well; that is how they *ought to be.*[102]

THE FINAL CAUSE OF AN OBJECT IS FOR AN OBJECT TO DO WHAT IT IS DOING WELL.

The Argument from the Subjectivity of Rights

ARGUEMENT FROM THE SUBJECTIVITY OF RIGHTS!

The Argument from the Subjectivity of Rights holds that the important thing is not the natural law, but personal rights that shield me from the natural law. The natural law forbids taking innocent life—I protest that I have a right to free reproductive decisions. The natural law directs the use of the sexual powers—I protest that I have a right to free sexual expression. So it is that the roster of subjective rights becomes a wish list; if I want something badly enough, I think I have a right to it.

In American jurisprudence, this movement reached its apex in the "mystery passage" of *Planned Parenthood v. Casey* (1992),[103] which haughtily asserts a "right to define one's own concept of existence, of meaning, of the universe, and of the mystery of human life." The passage doesn't quite reject the idea of a higher law. What it does is affirms a degenerate conception of higher law; it incoherently tries to make a higher-law principle of freedom from higher law principles.

The fact that this principle is incoherent ought to deprive it of force, for there is no coherent way to apply an incoherency. Unfortunately it does have force, because it is applied inconsistently. *Casey* itself upheld abortion; reasoning from the mystery passage, the plurality concluded that is up to me to "define" whether my unborn child exists, has meaning, has a place in the universe, or counts as a human life. Logically, it should have

---

102. In logic, the way to express this point is to distinguish between predicative and attributive adjectives. "Red" is an example of a predicative adjective; it means the same thing no matter what kind of thing we are talking about. By contrast, "fast" is an example of an attributive adjective; what it means depends on what kind of thing we are talking about. As Peter Geach points out, the adjective "good" is attributive. See Peter Geach, "Good and Evil," *Analysis* 17 (1956), pp. 33-42.

103. 505 U.S. 833 (1992).

concluded that it is also up to me to "define" whether my next-door neighbor exists, has meaning, has a place in the universe, or counts as a human life. It doesn't, but the only possible explanation is that it is only at war with babies, not next-door neighbors. The argument might go like this: Citizens have an unchallengeable right to conduct their lives according to their own subjective definitions of reality, but judges have an unchallengeable power to decide what counts as a definition. The effect of this little maneuver is that everyone must define reality as the judges do; they have used the language of absolute subjective liberty in order to buttress absolute judicial tyranny. Submission to the natural law, discovered, not invented, not changeable to suit our whims, would have made such tyranny impossible. According to subjectivism, however, *that* is the meaning of tyranny.

The problem lies not with the idea that people have rights. They do. The older natural law thinkers did not talk much about rights, but they could have; after all, if I have a duty not to murder you, then by implication you have a right not to be murdered. Note well that in this way of thinking, the rights of the "subject," of the individual, are grounded on an *objective* order of right and wrong. The problem with contemporary rights talk is that it denies the necessity of such grounding; rights seem to float in midair. If no grounding is necessary, then there is no limit to what can be asserted as a right. "Everything is permitted," declares the judge, "but I get to say what 'everything' includes."

The Argument from the Relativity of Morals
Moral relativism maintains that the natural law cannot exist because morality is different everywhere. In philosophy, the most influential recent advocate of relativism is Richard Rorty, who writes, "I do not think there are any plain moral facts out there in the world, nor any truths independent of language, nor any neutral ground on which to stand and argue

that either torture or kindness are preferable to the other."[104]
In jurisprudence, its most influential recent advocate is
Richard A. Posner, judge of the U.S. Court of Appeals for the
Seventh Circuit. No babe in the woods, Posner knows better
than to flatly deny the reality of moral universals; all cultures
recognize the wrong of such things as murder. Conceding the
point, Posner goes on to trivialize it. He denies not that there
are moral universals, but that there are "interesting" moral
universals:

> [M]orality is local. There are no interesting moral uni-
> versals. There are tautological ones, such as "Murder is
> wrong" where "murder" means "wrongful killing," and
> there are a few rudimentary principles of social coop-
> eration—such as "Don't lie all the time" or "Don't
> break promises without any reason" or "Don't kill your
> relatives or neighbors indiscriminately"—that may be
> common to all human societies. If one wants to call
> these rudimentary principles the universal moral law,
> fine; but as a practical matter, no moral code can be
> criticized by appealing to norms that are valid across
> cultures, norms to which the code of a particular cul-
> ture is a better or worse approximation. These norms,
> the rudimentary principles of social cooperation that I
> have mentioned, are too abstract to serve as standards
> for moral judgment.[105]

The argument may be put like this: Principles like "Don't
murder," "Don't lie," and "Don't break promises" may seem to
say something, but this is an illusion. "Murder" means merely
"wrongful killing," so "Murder is wrong" translates to "Killing
is wrong *when it is wrong to kill.*" "Lie" means merely "wrongful

---

104. Richard Rorty, *Contingency, Irony, and Solidarity* (Cambridge: Cambridge
     University Press. 1989), p. 173.
105. Richard A. Posner, "The Problematics of Moral and Legal Theory." *Harvard
     Law Review*, Vol. 111 (1998), p. 1637.

falsehood," so "Lying is wrong" translates to "It is wrong to tell *those falsehoods that it is wrong to tell.*" "Promise" means only "vow it is wrong to break," so "Breaking promises is wrong" translates to "It is wrong to break vows *that it is wrong to break.*" In each case, all that we are really being told is "It is wrong to do what it is wrong to do." True, there is a rudimentary agreement across cultures that at least it is *sometimes* wrong to kill, to tell falsehoods, and to break vows. But concerning the substance of the matter—*when* it is wrong to do these things—there is no agreement whatsoever. The supposed universals turn out to be mere tautologies; they say literally nothing.

Now this is an empirical claim, and as such, it invites investigation. Posner sees the invitation coming and heads it off by sheer assertion. As he obviously knows, natural lawyers would say that discordancy among cultures about killing, telling falsehoods, and breaking vows conceals an underlying unity. There exist certain universal norms—discovered, not invented—from which the codes of particular cultures may deviate in various ways, but to which they are better or worse approximations. Posner asserts as a given that this is not true. But it is not a given; it is precisely what we are trying to ascertain. Are there in fact implicit norms to which the codes of particular cultures are better or worse approximations? Let's consider Posner's first case, murder.

According to the natural law tradition, there is indeed an implicit norm concerning murder: That we must never deliberately take innocent human life. This is far different from the tautology that killing is wrong when killing is wrong, for it specifies *when* killing is wrong. Consider a difficult case: Cannibalism. It may seem that the cannibal thinks it is all right to deliberately take innocent human life, but it is much more likely that he concedes the point and denies that the people in the other tribe are human (or perhaps that they are innocent).

If I were Judge Posner, I might reply as follows: "Granted what you call the implicit norm, you have merely substituted an elaborate tautology for a simple one. A human is merely a being such that deliberately taking his life, when he is innocent, is wrong. Therefore, your so-called implicit norm translates, 'It is wrong to deliberately take the lives of innocent beings *whose lives, when they are innocent, it is wrong to take.*' Just as before, you are saying precisely nothing."

Not so. The natural law position does not substitute an elaborate tautology for a simple one; on the contrary, the reply substitutes an elaborate unproved assertion for a simple one. This time it takes as a given that there is no implicit norm concerning *what counts as human* to which the codes of particular cultures are better or worse approximations. But again, this is not a given but rather the thing we are trying to ascertain. Now consider: If there really were no implicit norm concerning what is human, then it would be impossible to argue with cannibals about the matter. Experience shows that this is not true, for various cannibal tribes have yielded to the persuasion of missionaries and others. Consider too, that unless the cannibal knows deep down that the people in the other tribe are human, it is difficult to explain why he performs elaborate expiatory rituals before taking their lives.

Besides, in real life, relativism is always more or less a fraud. No relativist ever applies his relativism consistently; either he is a selective relativist (that is, a selective moralist), or else a smokescreen artist—using relativism as cover for a pet moral theory that pretends to be something else. Judge Posner is both a selective relativist *and* a smokescreen artist. His pet moral theory is "adaptationism," the view that the promotion of a society's subjective goals is an objective good. In his own words, "Relativism suggests an adaptationist conception of morality, in which morality is judged nonmorally—in the way a hammer might be judged well or poorly adapted to its function of hammering nails—by its contribution to the survival, or other goals, of a society."[106] On close examination he doesn't really believe in adaptationism either. He is merely a selective adaptationist.

---

106. Ibid.

Consider for example the line of moral reasoning advanced in his dissenting opinion in *Hope Clinic v. Ryan* (1999),[107] a case concerning partial-birth abortion. In view of the fact that large majorities oppose this gruesome practice, adaptationism would have bid him submit to the "social goal" of ending it. Instead he advanced a variety of arguments as to why this social goal was wrong, and the majority wrong to have held it.

Two Final Arguments

I discuss these last two arguments together, partly because they have been considered in previous chapters and partly because they work as a team. One, which we may call the Argument from Utter Ruin, maintains that man is so far fallen that his mind recoils from moral truth. The other, which we may call the Argument from the Written Word, maintains that Holy Scripture is the one and only place to find moral truth. Here, from William Einwechter, is an illustration of the former view:

> [T]he fall of man and the resultant curse upon nature make it impossible for natural law to be the standard for the moral law. Because of sin, man's reason and conscience have been corrupted; therefore, these cannot be reliable sources for the knowledge of right and wrong, justice and injustice.[108]

And here, from the same author, is a typical expression of the latter:

> Natural law theory is an "imagination" that exalts man's reason over God's revealed law-word. The church is called to demolish natural law speculation and bring all spheres of ethics (including the sociopolitical) under the authority of the Word of Christ....

---

107. 195 F.3d 857 (7th Cir. 1999).
108. William Einwechter, "Natural Law: A Summary and Critique." *The Christian Statesman* 42:1 (January-February, 1999).

In contrast to the abstract, unwritten, and imprecise
natural law which has to be unveiled by man's fallible
reason stands the Word of God. The Bible gives the
revelation of God's moral law with the precision of
written law. Biblical law is perfect, objective, compre-
hensive, detailed, and infallible..., giving man all the
knowledge he needs to answer all the moral questions
for every sphere of life...; it is the only sound basis for
ethics and for building a just and lasting civil order.[109]

If these two arguments are true, then reasoning with the unre-
generate man is futile; he cannot be reached that way. The only
possible way to persuade him on any point of right or wrong is to
expose him to the biblical word of God. As Einwechter puts it:

This darkened, carnal, foolish mind, this defiled conscience is the means of knowing and establishing the
moral law? Yes, says the theory of natural law. We say,
God forbid! The objective standard of God's own infallible Word alone can suffice to reveal His moral law.[110]

But both arguments are false. Although they claim to base
themselves on the Bible, in fact they are thoroughly unscriptural.

First, man is not *utterly* averse to moral truth. If he were, then
he could no more be reached by quoting the Bible than in any
other way. The Bible itself describes us as divided. We continue
to bear God's image, and His law is written on our hearts; on the
other hand we have stained that image, and we are uneasy about
the inscription. This is why Paul alludes to the "conflicting
thoughts" of the gentiles that "accuse or perhaps excuse them".
Beings who are torn in their thoughts may not listen to reason;
then again they may. Of course they often suppress their moral

TENSION
BETWEEN
TOTAL
DEPRAVITY
AND THE
IMAGE DEI

---

109. Ibid.
110. William Einwechter, "Natural Law: A Summary and Critique." *The Christian
    Statesman* 42:1 (January-February, 1999).

knowledge, pretending to themselves that they don't know what they really do. Even so, suppression is a different thing than ignorance, and beings who are suppressing their knowledge must be approached differently than beings who have no knowledge to suppress. Natural law theory tells us what is down there, so perchance we can dredge it up.

Second, the question is not whether there is a law *apart* from the law of God, but whether God has revealed His law in one way only. The answer is that there is a double revelation. One is special, for the community of faith; the other is general, for all mankind. This idea is not merely an invention of clever theologians, for as we have seen in chapter four, the Bible itself testifies to general revelation—in fact, to at least four modes of it. This is why the Christians of an earlier day spoke of the Book of Scripture and the Book of Nature, both from God. To be sure, the former book is more perfect. It tells us more, tells it more clearly, and goes on to explain the means of salvation. Even so, it doesn't start from scratch. You have to know general revelation to grasp what special revelation is talking about.

Finally, it is nonsense to say that the biblical way to speak with our neighbors is to beat them over the head with the Bible. Surely, if we wish to be biblical, we will follow the Bible's example, and the apostles did no such thing. When they spoke with fellow Jews, who accepted special revelation, they began with special revelation. But when they spoke with pagans, who were strangers to special revelation, they began with general revelation. "For as I passed along, and observed the objects of your worship, I found also an altar with this inscription...."[111] "[H]e did good and gave you from heaven rains and fruitful seasons...."[112] "As even some of your poets have said...."[113] The unbiblical innovation lies not in trying to reason with nonbelievers, but in refusing to make the attempt.

---

111. Acts 17:23 (RSV).
112. Acts 14:17 (RSV).
113. Acts 17:28 (RSV).

9 | How Not to Link the Natural Law with Legislation

I remarked in chapter six that human law is the application of the natural law, by public authority, to the circumstances of particular human societies. To reason correctly from general considerations of what is good and right *is* to apply the natural law, even if the theoretical term "natural law" is never used.

Sometimes people complain, "Morality should not be legislated." What they usually mean when they say this is that they want their view of what is right and good to be legislated in place of the traditional one. A law defining marriage as the union of a man and a woman rests on a certain moral view, and a law defining marriage as whatever you like rests on different one. In a sense, morality is the only thing that is ever legislated, for every law rests on some moral judgment—even if it rests on a false one. There are literally no counterexamples. Suppose the government mandates that users of a certain public road must pay a toll; the moral judgment in this case is probably that people owe a return for the benefits they receive. Or suppose the government establishes a tariff on imported steel; at some point a decision must have been reached that the economic costs of such a tariff are justified by its offsetting contributions to other aspects of the common good. I may believe that this conclusion is false, but I cannot deny that it expresses a moral judgment.

Sometimes people say that the law should be based on "utilitarian," "pragmatic," or "economic" rather than moral considerations. What they conveniently overlook is that utilitarianism, pragmatism, and what we may call economism are themselves moral theories—theories about the human good—however debased they may be. Classical utilitarianism defines the good as "happiness," with happiness defined narrowly as "pleasure."[114] Pragmatists define the good as "whatever works," with the answer to the question "works at doing what?" defined by the speaker.[115] Economism—a variety of materialism—defines the good as wealth.

The fact that every law proceeds from some moral view does not imply that every way of bringing moral judgments into law is right. There are limits. How can this be so? If we limit the introduction of moral judgments into law, doesn't that show that we aren't really serious about the natural law? On the contrary, certain limits are necessary *because* we are serious about the natural law. They arise from the very nature of the moral goods to be upheld. We are all familiar with such limits in our personal moral life. If I refuse to use bribery to win friends, the reason is not that I do not want friends, but that I do; for friends cannot be won by bribery, and the sort of companion that can be won by bribery is not a friend.

---

114. "The creed which accepts as the foundation of morals, Utility, or the Greatest Happiness Principle, holds that actions are right in proportion as they tend to promote happiness, wrong as they tend to produce the reverse of happiness. By happiness is intended pleasure, and the absence of pain; by unhappiness, pain, and the privation of pleasure." John Stuart Mill, *Utilitarianism*, Chapter 2; cf. Jeremy Bentham, *An Introduction to the Principles of Morals and Legislation*. For critique, see J. Budziszewski, *Written on the Heart: The Case for Natural Law* (Downers Grove, Illinois: InterVarsity, 1997), Chapters 10-12.

115. The motto "Whatever works" is consequentialist; it expresses the view that the ends justify the means, that anything whatsoever might be justified if the results are good enough. Utilitarianism is also consequentialist, but unlike utilitarianism, pragmatism does not supply the definition of the ends or results to be sought. People sometimes assume that the natural law tradition is consequentialist because of what Thomas Aquinas calls the first principle of practical reason, "good is to be done and pursued, and evil is to be avoided." This is a gross misunderstanding, because according to the natural law tradition, some acts are intrinsically evil, apart from results. This consequentialism denies.

Wrong Ways to Exercise Legislative Moral Judgment

Among other things, laws command. Among the most serious "wrong ways" of exercising moral judgment which legislators should avoid are commanding what cannot be seen, commanding more than common good requires, commanding without due regard for prudence, and commanding without due regard for what natural law thinkers call "subsidiarity."[116]

Courts also issue commands, and if such errors are committed in a judicial rather than a legislative context, then of course they are wrong there too. In most legislative systems, though, the legislature establishes the general rules that courts, coming afterward, apply to the circumstances of particular cases; therefore, the rules that courts devise to guide their own deliberation depend on what the legislature has already done. For certain special reasons, the American case is somewhat different. We will touch on this difference later.

Commanding What Cannot Be Seen

One limit on the way in which moral judgments may be brought into legislation was discussed briefly in chapter six: The law may command and prohibit outward actions, but it must not attempt to command or prohibit the hidden movements of the heart, such as virtues, vices, feelings, thoughts, and beliefs.[117] Consider the virtue of honesty, which is an interior disposition of character. The authorities may cultivate and encourage honesty in all sorts of indirect ways. For example, they may use the "bully pulpit" to commend it, or they may make perjury a punishable offense. Such methods are not only licit but laudable. But commending is different from commanding, and perjury is an outward act, which can be detected. By contrast, dishonest character is something hidden, which can only be inferred. If a

---

116. The corresponding idea in Reformed social thought is called "sphere sovereignty." Abraham Kuyper, the Reformed thinker who developed the idea of sphere sovereignty, acknowledged a debt to Pope Leo XIII, whose encyclical *Rerum Novarum* ("On the Condition of the Working Classes") (1891) stimulated reflection about subsidiarity.

117. Thomas Aquinas, *Summa Theologica*, I-II, Question 91, Article 4.

witness refrains from perjuring himself not from honesty but from fear or self-interest, the authorities will never know the difference. Therefore the law may never issue a command like "Be of honest character."

Commanding More than Common Good Requires

Law is ordained to the common, not the private good; that is why it has authority over everyone. Individuals can look after their private good by themselves, and the state has no authority to reach into their affairs when the common good is not affected. In fact, if we call to mind what a common good is—a good which is not diminished by being shared with others—the power of individuals to look after their affairs *is* a common good, which law should not only respect but promote. Far from being required by the natural law, then, paternalism is actually prohibited by it as contrary to human well-being.

Although this point may seem clear in the abstract, it is often misunderstood. Because there is a difference between private and common good, some people get the idea that there is a difference between "private virtues" which have no bearing on the common good, and "public virtues" which do. This is not the case. True, it impinges much more keenly on the public good when a citizen lies to the public than when he lies to his wife. However, both lies arise from the same wretched twist of character. There is not one virtue of public truthfulness and another virtue of private truthfulness; rather there is one virtue of truthfulness that is exercised in various acts, some of which are public and some of which are not. Now every virtue contributes to the common good. On the other hand, not every *act* of every virtue contributes significantly to the common good. Those which do may be commanded by law, but those which do not may not. Thus, the law properly takes an interest in whether a witness has been truthful in court, but it does not ordinarily take an interest in whether a teenager has been truthful in her secret diary.[118]

---

118. Thomas Aquinas, *Summa Theologica*, I-II, Question 96, Article 3.

A second confusion comes down to us from John Stuart Mill. In *On Liberty*, Mill grasped that an act or omission which does no significant harm to the common good is not a proper concern of law. His only original contribution was to vastly inflate the class of such acts, treating numerous lines of conduct as though they have no effect on others, even though they plainly do.[119] He accomplished this inflation in two ways. First, he ignored the social context in which acts take place. Whether I harm others by motorcycling without a helmet, for example, depends on various things like whether I have a family that depends on me for love, counsel, and financial support, whether I pool my risks through insurance, and whether those who witness my accident consider themselves bound to give me aid. The more extensive a society's network of mutual obligations, the more likely it is that others will be affected by what I do. Second, he employs various definitional tricks, so that when it suits him to do so he counts harm to important customs as not a harm, the harm of corrupting others as not a harm, harm to which a person consents as not a harm, the harm of giving offense as not a harm, the harm of destroying one's abilities to fulfill obligations to others as not a harm, and the risk of harm, distributed in such a way that we do not know on whom the sword will fall, as not a harm. Rather than aiding deliberation, these maneuvers short-circuit it.

Commanding Without Due Regard for Prudence

In chapter six I also mentioned two prudential reasons why not all acts of vice can be prohibited—two reasons why indiscriminate prohibition of everything that is wrong may end up doing more harm than good. The first reason was that if you indiscriminately pull up all the weeds, you may uproot some shoots of wheat along with them.[120] Consider liberty of discussion. The public

---

119. My comments here are the conclusions of a longer discussion of the harm principle in J. Budziszewski, *True Tolerance* (New Brunswick, N.J.: Transaction Publishers, 1992), pp. 18-24.

120. Thomas Aquinas, *Summa Theologica*, I-II, Question 91, Article 4.

square can be a disturbing place; some of the opinions aired are not only false but deeply disordered. On the other hand, if they were made legally unmentionable, then the arguments against them would become unmentionable too. Truth is sharpened and clarified in contest with error, and this advantage would be lost. For this reason discussion should probably be free except in certain narrowly defined cases, such as obscenity, defamation, and fighting words, which are not really about the presentation of arguments anyway.

The second reason was that although law indirectly seeks to promote good character, it must not attempt to lay upon citizens greater burdens than they can bear, for if it does, imperfect men will "break out into yet greater evils."[121] An example commonly given is Prohibition, when the attempt to suppress drunkenness by banning the sale of alcohol led to a vast black market with various associated problems. Actually the example is less obvious than it seems. According to Joseph Califano, a former U.S. health and welfare secretary, per capita alcohol consumption during Prohibition dropped by 50 percent, mental hospital admissions for alcoholic psychosis by 60 percent, and drunk and disorderly arrests by 50 percent. Welfare agencies dealt reported fewer alcohol-related family cases, and deaths from impure alcohol did not increase. Homicide rates rose, but at a slower rate than before Prohibition.[122] The two-sidedness of the Prohibition case illustrates the necessity for proceeding with caution. Not every case is the same.

Commanding Without Due Regard for Subsidiarity

I commented in chapter six that the Church has different work than the state, work which the law must respect. This principle may be generalized. The potentialities of man's created social nature unfold in not one or two but a multitude of

---

121. Thomas Aquinas, *Summa Theologica*, I-II, Question 96, Article 2.
122. Joseph Califano, "Fictions and Facts About Drug Legalization," *America* 174:9 (March 16, 1996), p. 7.

different forms of solidarity or association. Each of these—family, Church, neighborhood, workers' association, and so forth—has its own mission or calling, its own proper purposes, which the law should seek neither to take over nor absorb. Indeed it has no authority to do so, for no such conquest would genuinely promote the common good; the state exists for the sake of civil society, not civil society for the state. Rather than pushing the various forms of human association aside or doing their work in their place, the state should see to the background conditions that they need in order to flourish. It follows that whatever these forms of association can do themselves, law should allow and encourage them to do. This is the principle of subsidiarity.

Although the insight behind subsidiarity has very old roots, natural law thinkers did not systematize the principle until the nineteenth century, and it did not acquire its name until the twentieth.[123] There is a reason why it blossomed when it did. Subsidiarity is the antidote to a pair of temptations that grew dangerously strong during the industrial revolution and remain powerful today. Traditional societies like as families, guilds, and villages were being pulled part. It seemed as though nothing would be left but a solid lump of government on the one hand and a gas of unrelated individuals on the other. One of the resulting temptations was to deny the common good in the name of the individual; the other was to pervert the common good by subordinating that individual to the state. Subsidiarity cuts a path between these two errors by exalting the work and proper rights of all of the "little platoons" that grow up between the state at the top and the individual at the bottom.

---

123. Its name comes from the Latin word *subsidium*, which means "a help." "Just as it is gravely wrong to take from individuals what they can accomplish by their own initiative and industry and give it to the community, so also it is an injustice and at the same time a grave evil and disturbance of right order to assign to a greater and higher association what lesser and subordinate organizations can do. For every social activity ought of its very nature to furnish help [*subsidium*] to the members of the body social, and never destroy and absorb them." Pope Pius XI, *Quadragesimo Anno* ("On Reconstruction of the Social Order"), 79 (1931).

A number of different lines of reasoning converge on subsidiarity. The heart of the idea is that the various forms of association have callings and rights of their own, so the most direct route to the principle is to consider the calling and rights of a particular form of association, then generalize. I introduced the principle above by beginning with the Church. For Thomas Aquinas, the stimulus to reflection was the embattled new mendicant orders.[124] For Leo XIII, it was workingmen's unions.[125] For the contemporary homeschool movement, it is the family.

---

124. Thomas Aquinas, *Contra impugnantes Dei cultum et religionem* ("An Apology for the Religious Orders").

125. Pope Leo XIII, *Rerum Novarum* ("On Labor and Capital").

10 | How Not to Link the Natural Law with Jurisprudence

In the previous chapter I commented that in most legislative systems, the legislature establishes general rules, which courts, coming afterward, apply to the circumstances of particular cases. This makes the rules that courts devise to guide their own deliberation depend on what the legislature has already done. American jurisprudence provides an exception, because the Constitution limits what the legislature may do, and the courts claim the final say in interpreting the Constitution.

It is most implausible that the Framers actually intended courts to have the final say, because the Constitution is quite explicit about legislative checks on the judiciary. All courts except the Supreme Court are established by Congress and can be abolished by Congress. The size and composition of the Supreme Court itself are Congressional decisions. Congress can make regulations about the Supreme Court's appellate jurisdiction, and can even declare exceptions to it. Finally, it can remove judges from office for misbehavior. How then has it been possible for the judiciary to get away with the extravagant claim of an exclusive authority to say what the Constitution means? What the Framers overlooked is the fact that although they had given legislators strong checks against the judiciary, they had also unwittingly given them a powerful incentive not to make use of these checks. The reason: Legislators periodically face the electorate, while judges do not. Thus, legislators who want to be re-elected have a motive to hand off politically sensitive issues to the courts, which may be only too happy to decide them. Consequently, the rules that the courts devise to guide their interpretation of the Constitution— for that matter, even its interpretations of statutes—may often function more like laws than laws do.

Wrong Ways to Exercise Judicial Moral Judgment

Except for the usurpation of the legislature's role, everything that courts do wrong when they exercise moral judgment can be done wrong by legislatures too. However, certain kinds of transgressions have been more conspicuous in recent jurisprudence than in recent legislation. The chief of these are asserting moral judgment gratuitously; asserting as a moral judgment what is really an imperious emotion; asserting *bad* moral judgment; and asserting a defective *theory* of moral judgment.

Asserting Moral Judgment Gratuitously

I argued in chapter five that courts should defer to legislatures concerning the remote implications of the natural law. Legislatures are designed for discerning these remote implications, and fashioning them into general rules; courts are designed for the very different work of adjudication. For example, legislatures have the power of initiative. They take up whatever issues they deem important, whereas courts consider only cases and controversies brought to them by others. Another difference is that legislatures consider all possible conditions, both actual and possible, whereas courts focus on the circumstances of the case at hand. Finally, the legislature in a system like ours depends on the approbation of the entire body of voters, whereas courts depend on the approbation of narrow and self-reinforcing experts, the views of whom may depart widely from the common moral sense of the plain person. What good lawmaking requires is wide-spectrum practical wisdom. Good adjudication requires more tightly focused virtues, such as the capacity to perceive relevant differences between different cases in order to know which principle or precedent to apply.

Do these facts imply that judges should not exercise moral judgment at all? No, there are two sorts of moral judgment that they may exercise without wrong. First comes <u>the routine sort</u>—the sort that is inseparable from statutory construction. A judge is often forced to fall back on the natural law simply to grasp what the positive law means. In chapter five I borrowed an example from Professor Charles E. Rice. Consider another. Among other things, the Fourteenth Amendment prohibits the states from making or enforcing any laws which deny to persons within their jurisdiction the "equal protection of the laws." What is meant by equal protection? There are several possible answers to this question, but none of them can be defended without a certain moral intelligence. Suppose we construe the meaning of the clause narrowly, as whatever the framers of the Fourteenth Amendment had in mind. What they had in mind was protecting the newly-freed slaves from arbitrary discrimination. Very well, but the clause does not actually limit its reach to slaves—it says "persons." Are any other classes of persons relevantly similar to newly-freed slaves? Or consider the next few words of the interpretation. Not all discrimination is arbitrary; it makes sense to deny the vote to twelve-year-olds. Arbitrary discrimination is discrimination without a good reason. But what counts as a good reason? Such questions cannot be answered without moral judgment. We may seek to evade the necessity, perhaps by saying, "What counts as relevantly similar is what the framers of the Fourteenth Amendment would have considered relevantly similar," or "What counts as a good reason is what the framers of the Fourteenth Amendment would have counted as a good reason," but the framers of the Fourteenth Amendment did not exhaustively answer all such questions. They could not have. Even if our wish is to defer to *their* moral judgment, we must exercise *our* moral judgment to discern what their judgment probably was.

The second kind of moral judgment that judges may exercise without reproach is the non-routine kind. This is the kind that steels martyrs. Every now and then a republic degenerates into a tyranny, as the Weimar Republic descended into the abyss of Naziism. On such an occasion the legislature may enact decrees which violate the natural law not subtly but blatantly. During the Third Reich, Jews were sent in millions to their deaths for no other reasons than that they were Jews. Now the wrong of deliberately taking innocent human life is not a remote implication of the natural law, so that on such a point the judge ought to defer to the moral judgment of the legislature; it is one of those things that all human beings know. Because a legislative decree that defies it is not a true law but an act of violence masquerading as a law, in such a case the judicial oath to uphold the laws does not apply. The judge may resign—or, if he has the courage to die as a witness to truth, he may place himself in the way of the regime and be an obstacle.

The problem lies not with these two kinds of judicial moral judgment, but with all others. Too many judges usurp moral judgments that really do belong to the legislature. Such arrogance must always be condemned.

Asserting as a Moral Judgment What Is Really an Imperious Emotion

Feelings and emotions certainly have something to do with moral judgment. As Aristotle remarked, a person of good character feels things like fear, confidence, appetite, anger, and pity "at the right times, with reference to the right objects, towards the right people, with the right motive, and in the right way."[126] We often have the feeling that something is morally suspect long before we understand why it is. "I can't tell what's wrong," we say, "but something smells fishy."

---

126. Aristotle, *Nicomachean Ethics* 2.6, trans. W.D. Ross. I am using the Internet Classics Archive at http://classics.mit.edu .

But there are at least three problems with following feelings. The first is that not everyone's sense of moral smell is equally good. To a bad person, even holiness smells bad.[127] The second is that the sense of moral smell is nearly incommunicable, and to the extent that it can be communicated, a bad sense of moral smell is easier to communicate than a good one. Even a mediocre novelist can make adultery smell heavenly, but it takes a writer of genius to convey the smell of heaven to adulterers. The third is that in the final analysis, moral judgment is a function of the intellect, not the feelings. Feelings may prime the pump, but they are not what moral judgment *is*.[128]

Unfortunately, capricious judges often treat feelings and judgment as the same thing. Having expressed their emotions about a case with great indignation, they seem to think that they have delivered an unanswerable dictum, binding on everyone else. In effect, they are presenting themselves as persons of such perfect virtue that their feelings can be trusted as reasonable even when they have no reasons to go with them.

An illustration of imperious emotion masquerading as moral judgment may be found in the opinion of Justice Blackmun, dissenting from the opinion of the majority in *DeShaney v. Winnebago County* (1989).[129] The facts of the case are as follows. A series of suspicious injuries to four-year-old Joshua led the county department of social services to conclude that he was being beaten by his father. After a series of interventions and a series of further suspicious injuries, the father one day beat the

---

127. "For we are the aroma of Christ to God among those who are being saved and among those who are perishing, to one a fragrance from death to death, to the other a fragrance from life to life." 2 Corinthians 2:14-15, RSV.

128. The philosopher Yves R. Simon goes so far as to suggest that in a person of good character who is not misled by wishes that "are not what they are supposed to be," the assent of the intellect to the sense of moral smell is real knowledge, which he calls "knowledge by inclination." Most natural law thinkers think the matter is not so clear as Simon makes out, and even Simon concedes that it is better to have "knowledge by cognition" if you can get it— knowledge backed up by rational demonstrations. Yves R. Simon, *The Tradition of Natural Law: A Philosopher's Reflections* (New York: Fordham University Press, 1965), pp. 126-136.

129. 489 U.S. 189 (1989).

child so terribly that he suffered profound brain injury, requiring his confinement to an institution for the rest of his life. On the boy's behalf, his mother argued that by undertaking to protect the boy, the county social services department had acquired an "affirmative duty"[130] protect him. Having failed to protect him, the department should be viewed as having deprived the boy of liberty without due process of law—thereby violating the Due Process Clause of the Fourteenth Amendment.

For present purposes, let us pass over the unhappy question whether "substantive due process," on which the Court relied, makes sense. The incoherencies of this particular notion are not germane to the problem I am illustrating.[131] Before the Court was the question whether the actions of the state toward the boy really had generated an affirmative duty to protect him. To decide the issue, it compared the circumstances of the case with the circumstances of previous cases in which state actions toward individuals had been held to generate such duties. For example, the Court had held in *Estelle v. Gamble* (1976)[132] that by incarcerating a prisoner, a state acquires a duty to provide medical care: "it is but just that the public be required to care for the prisoner, who cannot, by reason of the deprivation of his liberty, care for himself." What the Court had to do was decide whether the actions of the county social services officials in *DeShaney* were relevantly similar to the actions of state officials in cases like *Estelle*.

I note in passing that this is a moral question. *DeShaney* is relevantly similar to cases like *Estelle* if it is similar in the ways that are relevant to acquiring duties. It is futile to say that we

---

130. What the Court means by an "affirmative" duty is what ethical philosophers call a "positive" duty—a duty to do something, as contrasted with a duty not to do something.

131. "Due process" means nothing but "proper procedure." The Due Process Clause, therefore, is a procedural limit on *how* certain enumerated things may be taken away, not a substantive limit on *which* of them may be taken away. I am not suggesting that the Constitution does not impose limits of the latter sort, only that it doesn't impose them here.

132. 429 U.S. 97 (1976).

are speaking of legal rather than moral duties, for legal duty is a special case of moral duty. To ask whether the state had a legal duty to protect the endangered boy is to ask whether it had a *moral* duty to do so, of the type enforceable by higher authority, under conditions which included the existence of certain laws and precedents. Now there is simply no way to determine whether the cases were relevantly similar just by looking at them. The judge must bring intelligence to bear, and the species of intelligence required is the one which distinguishes between what does have bearing on question of moral duty, and what does not.

According to the majority, the cases were not relevantly similar. The Court reasoned that in each of its precedents, the reason why the state had a duty to do something for an individual was that it had deprived that individual of the ability to do it for himself. Although the boy had been deprived of certain capacities in *DeShaney* too, he had been deprived of them by his father, not by the state. Now the Fourteenth Amendment forbids the state from taking away life, liberty, or property without due process of law, but it does not guarantee a certain level of security against the invasion of these goods by private parties—as though it could promise ahead of time that its efforts to provide protection would never fail. Still, it might be argued that the state had not tried *hard enough* to protect the citizens. The problem here is that the Court lacks the resources for defining how hard is hard enough. The common law of tort might offer such resources, but that is for the state legislature to decide. Certainly no such resources are available in the Fourteenth Amendment, for had the state functionaries acted too quickly to remove the boy from the custody of his father, "they would likely have been met with charges of improperly intruding into the parent-child relationship, charges based on the same Due Process Clause that forms the basis for the present charge of failure to provide adequate protection."

Justice Blackmun's dissent is of an entirely different character. He asserts gross negligence on the part of the state functionaries, but he misrepresents what they actually did.[133] He
says they should have done more, but he fails to say what they
should have done or how he knows. The essence of his argument is a denunciation of argument and an exaltation of his own
righteous feelings. Calling attention to the Court's distinction
between positive and negative duties—duties to do and duties
not to do—he complains:

> [S]uch formalistic reasoning has no place in the inter-
> pretation of the broad and stirring Clauses of the
> Fourteenth Amendment. Indeed, I submit that these
> Clauses were designed, at least in part, to undo the for-
> malistic legal reasoning that infected antebellum
> jurisprudence.... Like the antebellum judges who
> denied relief to fugitive slaves... the Court today
> claims that its decision, however harsh, is compelled by
> existing legal doctrine.[134]

Such statements are merely libel; the problem with the
antebellum arguments which denied relief to fugitive slaves was
not that they were "formalistic" but that they were wrong.
What Justice Blackmun really means when he objects to "formalistic" reasoning is that he objects to *principled* reasoning, and
he objects to it on no other grounds than that it checks the
warm flood of his pity:

---

133. Justice Blackmun writes that county social services employees did "essentially
nothing except, as the Court revealingly observes, ante, at 193, 'dutifully
recorded these incidents in their files.'" In fact, as the Court details, in the beginning they did a good deal more than keep records. The difficulty lay in collecting
enough evidence of child abuse to retain the boy in the custody of the juvenile
court, and over time they became more passive. Even so, they pressured the boy's
father to enter into an agreement in which he promised to enroll the boy in a
preschool program, have his girlfriend move out of the home, and accept coun-
seling. Because the agreement was voluntary, they were unable to compel him to
comply. *Estelle v. Gamble*, Justice Blackmun, dissenting.
134. Ibid.

[T]he question presented by this case is an open one, and our Fourteenth Amendment precedents may be read more broadly or narrowly depending upon how one chooses to read them. Faced with the choice, I would adopt a "sympathetic" reading, one which comports with dictates of fundamental justice and recognizes that compassion need not be exiled from the province of judging.[135]

Justice Blackmun writes the foregoing sentences as though the question were whether or not to have compassion. On the contrary, the question regarding compassion is nearly always what to do with it once we've got it. If it moves us to help someone who is suffering, that is good. If it moves us to make someone else help him, that may or may not be good—depending. If we are moved by it to blame someone who is not to blame, that is bad. But these are the kinds of distinction that Blackmun blasts as "formalistic." What matters to him is not whether he is doing the right thing with his sympathy, but whether it "comforts" him, for as he continues (quoting a psychiatrist):[136]

We will make mistakes if we go forward, but doing nothing can be the worst mistake. What is required of us is moral ambition. Until our composite sketch becomes a true portrait of humanity we must live with our uncertainty; we will grope, we will struggle, and our compassion may be our only guide and comfort.

"Poor Joshua!" exclaims Justice Blackmun, "... abandoned by respondents who... did essentially nothing." Poor citizens! Ruled by imperial judges who cannot tell the difference between an argument and a gush of angry feelings.

---

135. Ibid.
136. Alan A. Stone, M.D., *Law, Psychiatry, and Morality: Essays and Analysis* (Arlington, Virginia: American Psychiatric Publishing, 1984), p. 262.

Asserting a Bad Moral Judgment,
or a Defective Theory of Moral Judgment

The last two wrong ways to bring moral judgment into law may be treated together, using the same examples. If only the courts distinguished properly between moral judgments that are their business and moral judgments that are not, these two errors would do much less damage. Unfortunately courts show little interest in doing so. This makes it all the more important for other parties to do so—including lawyers.

The most conspicuous recent judicial illustrations of both bad moral judgment and defective theory about moral judgment are a pair of Supreme Court cases involving homosexuality. In *Romer v. Evans* (1996),[137] the Court struck down an amendment to the Colorado state constitution that prohibited special preferences for homosexuals.[138] Although the amendment banned only discrimination in favor of homosexuals, the Court bizarrely construed it as discriminating against them. Even more important is *Lawrence v. Texas* (2003),[139] in which the Court invalidated a Texas statute prohibiting persons of the same sex from engaging in acts of sodomy. The twists and turns of the arguments presented by the Court concerning the Due Process and Equal Protection clauses do not concern us here, but their underlying moral themes do. These seem to be seven in number:

1. The ability to make sexual decisions of every sort— whether marital or non-marital, heterosexual or homosexual, sodomitical or non-sodomitical—is a "liberty"

---

137. 517 U. S. 620 (1996).

138. Here is its text: "Neither the State of Colorado, through any of its branches or departments, nor any of its agencies, political subdivisions, municipalities or school districts, shall enact, adopt or enforce any statute, regulation, ordinance or policy whereby homosexual, lesbian or bisexual orientation, conduct, practices or relationships shall constitute or otherwise be the basis of or entitle any person or class of persons to have or claim any minority status, quota preferences, protected status or claim of discrimination. This Section of the Constitution shall be in all respects self-executing."

139. 539 U.S. 558 (2003).

of such "transcendent dimensions" that it rises to
Constitutional status and demands the protection of
the courts. (*Lawrence.*)

2. Included in such liberty is a "right to demand
respect" for the sexual behavior that is chosen. The law
should not in any way associate it with "stigma."
(*Lawrence.*)

3. The fact that the governing majority has tradition-
ally viewed a particular sexual behavior as "immoral
and unacceptable" does not constitute rational grounds
for prohibiting it. (*Lawrence.*)

4. Neither does "respect for the traditional family."
(*Lawrence.*)

5. In fact, "Absent injury to a person or abuse of an
institution the law protects," no "rational basis" for
laws that regulate these matters can be imagined.
(*Lawrence, Romer.*)

6. Whether such laws distinguish among behaviors, or
distinguish among persons on the basis of behaviors,
the only possible explanation for them is sheer irra-
tional prejudice, or "animus." (Implied in *Lawrence*,
explicit in *Romer.*)

7. By implication, the traditional judicial doctrine that
the welfare of the community includes not only its
security, health, and safety, but also its morals—so that
the state can make and enforce reasonable regulations
concerning all these things—is simply wrong.

So it is that in seven short years, the span of time between
Romer and *Lawrence*, the natural law basis for judgments about

marriage, family, and sex is swept away and replaced with something that looks suspiciously like a religion of sex. "Religion" is not too strong a word, for not only does sexual license have "transcendent dimensions" in the eyes of the Court, but it turns out to be one of those things that "define the attributes of personhood."

Although the introduction of this religion is carried out in the name of "rational basis analysis," curiously little rationality is in evidence. The Court does not refute natural law arguments; it simply never mentions them. Nor does it mention the public health aspects of homosexual behavior.[140] Nor does it advance arguments for its own views of sex; it simply asserts them.

As though all this were not bad enough, the Court's theory of moral judgment is as bad as its moral judgment. Viewing "morality" as a prejudice, grounded in animus, that cannot offer a rational basis for law, it pushes "morality" aside. Yet it never seems to occur to the Court that its own view of sex constitutes a morality too. No wonder it doesn't reason well about morality; it doesn't understand what it is.

The antidote to bad moral judgment is good moral judgment, and the only antidote to a defective theory of judgment is a better one. We are well overdue for both.

Why a Certain Form of
Legal Positivism Is So Tempting

I have suggested that although certain kinds of moral judgment are a judge's business, other kinds are not. A judge who practices those other kinds is poaching; he is usurping the legislative prerogative. A more radical view suggests that this distinction does not go far enough. Instead it suggests that in the interests of judicial restraint, we should regard *all* moral judgments as prerogatives of the legislature.

---

140. This despite the fact that they had been laid out in detail in an *amicus* brief submitted to the Court by the Texas Physicians Resource Council, Christian Medical and Dental Association, and Catholic Medical Association.

The most interesting proponent of this view is U.S. Supreme Court Associate Justice Antonin Scalia. Justice Scalia accepts the legal positivist view of human law. Unlike many legal positivists, however, he believes in the natural law. What he rejects is the view that a judge may appeal directly to the natural law in support of his judgment of a case. As he sees it, the job of the judge is to do what the positive law commands, no more and no less, just as his oath of office demands. If the positive law commands him to do something evil, then he must simply resign, because he can no longer conscientiously fulfill his oath to uphold the law. Although Justice Scalia agrees that statutory construction may require judges to consult something beyond a statute's text, for him this something is not the natural law, but the "original understanding"—what the law would generally have been taken to mean at the time of its enactment. This is different from the "original intent," what the law meant subjectively to those who enacted it, because law is concerned with public meanings, not private ones.[141]

Justice Scalia is a good judge who deserves honor for wanting to rein in judicial caprice. His fear is that the instant we allow courts to appeal directly to the natural law, we give them a license to arrogate legislative authority to themselves. For who is to say what the natural law requires? Simply by declaring "The natural law says," a judge becomes unanswerable. I think I have already answered this objection by distinguishing, above and in chapter five, between the foundational precepts of the natural law, which judges know as well as legislators do, and the remote implications of the natural law, which legislatures are in a better position to discern than judges are. We have also seen that the practice of interpretation is literally inseparable from moral judgment. No matter how determined a judge may be to defer to the positive law, he must make tacit use of the natural law even to understand what the positive law is telling him.

---

141. See Antonin Scalia, *A Matter of Interpretation: Federal Courts and the Law* (Princeton, New Jersey: Princeton University Press, 1997). See also Antonin Scalia, "God's Justice and Ours," *First Things* 123 (May 2002), pp. 17-21.

But another argument can be made. If we examine Justice Scalia's theory of interpretation more closely we will see that it leads to the very conclusion that he is trying to stave off.

Notice first that Justice Scalia does not seek to banish *all* judicial thought of the natural law, but only a certain kind. In fact, certain kinds of judicial reliance on the natural law are assumed by his theory. Speaking in 2003 to a scholarly seminar on the natural law that I directed at the invitation of Calvin College, Justice Scalia graciously allowed the seventeen members of the seminar to press him on this point, and others, for several hours. His responses were challenging. If asked why a judge should keep his oath to uphold the law, he willingly conceded that the basis for this duty is the natural law precept that promises should be kept. He also conceded that grounding statutory construction in the "original understanding" of the statute leaves room for the possibility that the original understanding of a statute may have incorporated some idea of the natural law. But if all this is true, then what kind of judicial reliance on the natural law does his theory actually forbid?

To answer the question, two distinctions are necessary. Let us first distinguish between a law, the original understanding of which directs adherence to *some theory* of the natural law, and a law, the original understanding of which directs adherence to the natural law *as such*. Take for example the Contracts Clause, which forbids states from making laws "impairing the obligation of contracts."[142] What would the original understanding of the contracts clause have been? That is, what obligations would generally have been thought to arise from contracts at the time the clause was enacted? The original understanding of the obligations of contracts might have been something like "the obligations of contracts as we have learned of them from the natural law theories of our time," or it might have been something like "the actual obligations of contracts under the natural law, whatever they may be." In the first case, Justice Scalia's theory of

---

142. Article I, Section 10.

statutory construction would presumably require judges to consult writers like John Locke, Samuel Pufendorf, and Jean-Jacques Burlamaqui, while in the second case, it would require them to consult—what? apparently their own considered judgment of the natural law. The conclusion would seem to be inescapable. Someone might argue that the latter sort of original understanding never actually arises. But whether they do is an empirical question; the possibility cannot be ruled out *a priori*. So even according to Justice Scalia's theory, a judge might find himself compelled to consider the natural law *as such*.

Now let us make a second distinction. When a judge does appeal to the natural law *as such*, he might do so for the sort of reason just described—that is, because he is forced to do so by the original understanding of a statutory provision—or he might do so just because he thinks he should, independently of the original understanding of the statute. At least Justice Scalia's theory precludes the *latter* sort of appeal to the natural law, doesn't it? Surprisingly, no. Remember his answer to the question of *why* judges must appeal to original understanding rather than employing their personal judgment: They have taken an oath to uphold the laws. Given this reasoning, the actual wording of the oath becomes deeply important. Here is its wording as prescribed in 28 U.S. Code, Section 453:

> Oaths of justices and judges. Each justice or judge of the United States shall take the following affirmation before performing the duties of his office: 'I, _____, swear (or affirm) that I will administer justice without respect to equal right to the poor and to the rich, and that I will faithfully and discharge and perform all the duties incumbent upon me as _____ Constitution and laws of the United States. So help me God.'

It would seem that the oath militates against legal positivism, not for it. As it is worded, judges do not promise to administer justice *as defined* by the laws, but to administer justice *and* uphold the laws.

The meaning could hardly be more clear: Enacted law does not regulate the meaning of justice; rather justice regulates the meaning of enacted law. So the natural law tradition has always held.

A Final Word

As I close this book, I want to say a word about the social context of law. Barbarians are not met only on the Supreme Court; you know without my telling you how confused and skeptical most law students and professors are about morality. The same confusion and skepticism will meet you when you begin to practice law. Can you get through to skeptical colleagues? Does the natural law hold implications for breaking through the conversational barrier? I think it does.

A conversational natural law apologetic begins by calling the attention of colleagues to what they already know.

As I explained in chapter four, God Himself proceeded in this manner when He prefaced the Ten Commandments with a reminder of what He had done for them: "I am the LORD your God, who brought you out of Egypt, out of the land of slavery."[143] The point of the reminder was that the Hebrew people owed Him a debt of gratitude. Benefits imply obligation. But had He explicitly taught them this principle? No. The knowledge is factory equipment, inscribed upon the roots of our minds.

Paul proceeded in the same manner when he reminded the Athenians of their altar "TO AN UNKNOWN GOD." By doing so, he brought to the surface their cloudy awareness that despite their hundreds of idols, they had not found true deity. He followed through by explaining "What therefore you worship as unknown, this I proclaim to you."[144]

---

143. Exodus 20:2, RSV.
144. Acts 17:23, RSV.

Notice that although Paul made use of what I have called the four witnesses, he didn't waste time explaining the theory of the four witnesses. He simply relied upon the fact that they had already been whispering in the Athenians' ears. After all, it is the natural law which is written on their hearts, not the theory of the natural law.

There is a place for teaching the theory of the natural law, otherwise this book would have been futile. But your case is different. You're not the skeptic in the next office; you're the person trying to talk with him. With you I can get somewhere talking theory; with him I may not be able to. The problem isn't that he lacks the intelligence to understand it, but that it elicits a conditioned reflex he developed during law school—playing an intellectual game instead of trying to find the truth. So although you should be guided by theory, your words should remain at the level of common sense. Your goal isn't to push aside your colleague's common sense, but to elevate it.

In conversation about the hot button issue of marriage, for example, you might call attention to the fact that men and women seem to be made for each other. Something is missing in the man, which can only be completed by the woman. It is the same with her. Neither sex is complete in itself. Each needs the other. Everyone knows this. Only the most robotic ideologues deny it.

Or you might call attention to the fact that marriage is a procreative partnership, but that's not how you would put it. Among the products of our perverse educational system, the word "procreation" merely triggers another conditioned reflex. "Oh, yes. Natural teleology. Smart people don't believe in that, ergo, being smart, I don't." A certain common sense survives behind the conditioned reflex. Appeal to it directly. There is something special about marriage; it is the family-making institution, the only institution that can give a child a fighting chance of being raised by a mom and a dad.

The danger is that although the natural law is a real common ground, it's a slippery common ground. One reason is latency. People can know something about right and wrong without knowing that they know it. The other reason is denial. People can know something about right and wrong yet try *not* to know it. They may work desperately hard to convince themselves that they don't know what they really do. Honesty comes at too high a price. Of course the price of self-deception is higher still, but most people don't believe that.

A bad natural law apologetic ignores these difficulties; a good one anticipates them. It brings latent knowledge to the surface, dissipates smokescreens, and makes people aware of their self-deceptions.

Because we are at the end of the book, a single example must suffice.[145] Most abortion-minded women pretend to themselves that they are boxed in by circumstances; they say things like "I know abortion is wrong, but I just can't have a baby right now." How might you reply? My favorite crisis pregnancy counselor, who happens to be my wife, is very wise about natural law. She responds by simply asking, "What do you call what's in you?" Almost every pregnant woman—no matter what her conscious views about abortion—immediately and spontaneously replies, "I call it a baby." This makes it possible for the counselor to reply, "Then it sounds like you already have a baby. The question isn't whether to have one, but what you're going to do with the one you've already got."

The secret of her response is confidence in the reality of the law written on the other woman's heart. It brings her insight about natural law to bear in at least three ways: (1) She refuses to be distracted by the other woman's smokescreen. Instead she addresses herself to the human being hiding behind it.[146] (2) She doesn't try to pump new moral knowledge into the woman's mind. Instead she brings to the surface what the woman knows already. (3) She doesn't bring it to the surface by

---

145. I dicuss other examples in J. Budziszewski, *The Revenge of Conscience* (Dallas: Spence Publishing, 1999), Chapter 9.

146. For an even better example, see John 4:7-26.

telling the woman what she already knows. Instead she asks a question which elicits it.

As you see, natural law apologetics is like dredging the sunken conscience. It digs up suppressed moral knowledge and brings it to the surface, where it can do some good. The better you know what is down there, the better you are at digging it up.

The advantage that an understanding of natural law gives you in conversation with your skeptical colleagues is simply this: You know what they know better than they know what they know; you can draw out the knowledge they didn't know they had. This may be your *only* advantage, apart from reliance on God. But that is a great deal.

Appendix: Suggested Reading

The Classicus Locus

Aquinas, Thomas, *Treatise on Law* (same as *Summa Theologica*, I-II, Questions 90-108, esp. 90-97). Note, however, that the *Treatise on Law* is not self-contained, and was never intended to be read by itself, apart from the rest of the *Summa*.

The Best Twentieth Century Book on Natural Law

C.S. Lewis, *The Abolition of Man*. The one great drawback of this book is that the author tries to avoid the expression "natural law," using the expressions "Tao" and "the Way" in its place. This gives many readers the false impression that he endorsed the Eastern religion of Taoism.

The Man Who Ejected Natural Law from Twentieth-Century American Legal Education

Oliver Wendell Holmes, "Natural Law." *Harvard Law Review*, Vol. 62 (1918).

The Post-World War II Neo-Thomist Revival

Maritain, Jacques, *The Rights of Man and the Natural Law* and other works.

Simon, Yves R., *The Tradition of Natural Law: A Philosopher's Reflections* and other works.

Three Contemporary Anthologies

Cromartie, Michael, ed. *A Preserving Grace: Protestants, Catholics, and Natural Law*.

Forte, David F., ed., *Natural Law and Contemporary Public Policy.*

McLean, Edward B., ed., *Common Truths: New Perspectives on Natural Law.*

The "New Natural Law Theory" of Grisez and Finnis, Pro and Con

Germain G. Grisez, John Finnis, and Joseph Boyle, "Practical Principles, Moral Truth and Ultimate Ends." *American Journal of Jurisprudence* 32 (1987), pp. 99-151. (See also Finnis, *Natural Law and Natural Right*; Grisez, *Christian Moral Principles*, 3 vols.)

Hittinger, Russell, *A Critique of the New Natural Law Theory.*

Three Older Evaluations of Natural Law

Corwin, Edward S., *The "Higher Law" Background of American Constitutional Law.* This work is sometimes confused and must be read with caution.

D'Entreves, Alexander Passerin, *Natural Law: An Introduction to Legal Philosophy.*

Rommen, Heinrich A., trans. Thomas R. Hanley, intro. Russell Hittinger, *The Natural Law: A Study in Legal and Social History and Philosophy.*

The Present Outpouring of Work on Natural Law

Arkes, Hadley, *Natural Rights and the Right to Choose, Beyond the Constitution*, and other works.

Budziszewski, J., *What We Can't Not Know: A Guide*; *The Revenge of Conscience*; and *Written on the Heart: The Case for Natural Law.*

George, Robert P., *The Clash of Orthodoxies, In Defense of Natural Law*, and other works.

Hittinger, Russell, *The First Grace.* See also above.

Maritain, Jacques, *The Rights of Man and the Natural Law* and other works.

MacIntyre, Alasdair, "How Can We Learn What *Veritatis Splendor* Has to Teach?" *The Thomist* 58 (1994), pp. 171-195.

Novak, David. *Natural Law and Judaism* and *Covenantal Rights.* Concerning the Noahide Laws, which amount to a rabbinical natural law tradition, see also *The Image of the Non-Jew in Judaism.*

Rice, Charles E., *Fifty Questions on the Natural Law: What It Is and Why We Need It.*

Veatch, Henry, *Human Rights: Fact or Fancy?*

Another Brief Bibliography on Natural Law

From the Acton Institute, <http://www.acton.org/research/reading/natural_law.html> .

Natural Law for Lawyers
Order Form

Postal orders: Alliance Defense Fund
15333 N. Pima Road, Suite 165
Scottsdale, Arizona 85260

Telephone orders: 480-444-0020

Website orders: www.telladf.org

Please send *Natural Law for Lawyers* to:

Name: _____

Address: _____

City: _____ State: _____

Zip: _____ Telephone: (_____) _____

Book Price: $14.95

Shipping: $3.00 for the first book and $1.00 for each additional book to
cover shipping and handling within US, Canada, and Mexico.
International orders add $6.00 for the first book and $2.00 for
each additional book.

Or order from:
ACW Press
P.O. Box 110390
Nashville, TN 37222

(800) 931-BOOK

or contact your local bookstore